Freeman B. Dowd

The Temple of the Rosy Cross

The soul: its powers, migration, and transmigrations

Freeman B. Dowd

The Temple of the Rosy Cross
The soul: its powers, migration, and transmigrations

ISBN/EAN: 9783337038090

Printed in Europe, USA, Canada, Australia, Japan

Cover: Foto ©Thomas Meinert / pixelio.de

More available books at **www.hansebooks.com**

THE

TEMPLE OF THE ROSY CROSS.

THE SOUL:

ITS POWERS, MIGRATIONS, AND TRANSMIGRATIONS.

By F. B. DOWD.

"For these things that appear delight us, but make the things that appear not, hard to believe ; or the things that appear not are hard to believe."

PHILADELPHIA,
John R. Rue, Jr., Printer, No. 43 South Fourth Street.
—1 8 8 2.—

DEDICATION.

To JOHN HEANEY, of Buckley, Iroquois County, Illinois—him of the GREAT SOUL, LOFTY MIND, and LOVING HEART—" DOOR of the TEMPLE of the ROSY CROSS "—are these pages most respectfully and lovingly dedicated, by

THE AUTHOR.

PREFACE.

To provoke thought, and thus lift the world out of the rut into which it has fallen, the following pages have been written. The soul is no common or vulgar thing; and all approximation thereto, in thought, must be transcendental. This work claims to contain the fundamental *principles of all religions*—the PHILOSOPHY OF MAN-HOOD, and the road leading to a TRUE LIFE and IMMORTALITY, HERE, on this poor, much abused earth. "This is a matter-of-fact age," and "the day of miracles has passed." That is, those things which unaccountably happen, which were formerly ascribed to GOD, have come a little nearer home, and are now ascribed to NATURE. What satisfaction there is in a name, especially to child-ren! The superstition of the past, and of the stars, narrowed down to that of "the ape" and "the mud!" Instead of the facts of observation, I have attempted those of logic and common sense. DARWIN and HUXLEY have narrowed the mind down to a contem-plation of the mud "protoplasm," but I call you to a contemplation of man and his possibilities. *I came*, and found this beautiful earth fanned by the breath of deadly poison, which men, in the very agony of breathing, call life. *I go;* but in going, I would leave it a little purer for having been here. I am satisfied that man is the archi-tect of himself, and of all conditions, from "protoplasm" up; and it has been my effort to stir him upward to the creation of things worthy of himself. This year, 1881, is the close of an epoch in the world's history. It will, indeed, be sad, if we follow in the bloody track of our forefathers *downward*. We have now an opportunity, next year, of cutting loose the shackles that chain us to the corpse of the past. Shall we make the attempt? Reader, study these pages; the great ideas are merely shadowed, and are left crude and bare of detail, for you to clothe as your mind shall open to the grasping. Do not deny what I have written *without* a *full* and *clear comprehension* of the ideas.

It is not claimed that this work is *wholly* Rosicrucian. The sublime principles of this fraternity are not conveyed in this manner; but enough is given to enable the thoughtful and earnest searcher after truth to get a glimpse of the glory hidden, even now, as in the past. It is not the loud sounding bells of a sabbath morning, nor the roaring of organs and voices; neither is the high-toned oratory of the officiating priest, true worship; neither is it the *means*, however charming and gratifying, which move the infinite to the answering of prayer. Remember, "silence is strength;" noise confuses. It is "an empty sound," which silence comprehends not, or in the comprehension of it, loses it. The unwavering, persistent, incomprehensible (by us) thought, is the sustaining and *noiseless moving* power of the universe; and he who hath most of it is the most prayer-answering GOD, and in and by virtue thereof he is the greatest PRAYER.

F. B. DOWD.

(vi)

INTRODUCTION.

I. THE SUPERNATURAL.

In this matter-of-fact age the existence of GOD is seriously questioned by the greatest thinkers. The reason is obviously in the definitions which the religious world— more especially the Christian—gives to the term. The very nature of reason precludes the idea of the existence of a *Thing* above, separate and apart from the relationship of things. Reason cannot transcend its own source. That which is seen and known as nature—it being an infinitude of objects and phenomena—is considered as sufficient. And to reason and observation it does seem so. But if we undertake an analysis of this thing we call nature, we shall find it fully as remarkable and as contradictory as to suppose a Supreme Being as its maker. The antipathies of things show no *one* source. There seems, even to broad and deep reason, two principles at war with each other ; equally so to the fool they appear. One cannot be the cause of the other—nor can they be self-adjusting and regulating. Why? Because to us— not even to our reason —no *thing* is self-existent nor self-supporting. Everything in existence is dependent upon something else. If there is an exception to this, it *can-*

not be a THING. If we pass by things in our thought, and descend to principles, they also are dual and antagonistic. To suppose GOOD to be *the* principle, and evil its mere effect, is an absurdity, for one is as real as the other; and the evil is as much the cause of good as good is the cause of evil. We are so constituted that definitions are a necessity of all growth, intellectual as well physical. All nature is an effort to define itself. But what is it that is defining itself in this warfare of elements —this clashing of interests? Is it not something hidden away alike from feeling or observation and reason? The things or principles that clash are *patent*—we think we know them. All are conversant therewith, from the lowest worm that crawls to the loftiest intelligence; whether it be named PLEASURE and PAIN, or GOD and the DEVIL, or POSITIVE and NEGATIVE. But that something— which is struggling up out of the rock, water, air, and mud, into forms of beauty, use and deformity—as if to make itself known in multitudinous ways—what of it? Suppose we name it power! It is neither positive nor negative—neither good nor evil—but in the *definition* of *itself* becomes either good or bad, or indifferent. Power is that which supports all things, and we can well say it is neutral, for in itself there is no duality. . But pause a moment and think; even power has its antagonist— weakness! Is there the *weakness* of *nothing?* Is power limited to things, or even to principles? Again : where can weakness be found save in things? So power and weakness must be an attribute of things; but where they come from is unknown.

But what is a principle? If we can grasp a principle we have a foundation upon which to stand. It is as easy to define a thing as a principle. A principle is that which is self-existent. *There can be only one thing in existence* that is not derived from something else. What if it be a formless and boundless ocean! having nothing that can be predicated of things—neither fire nor that other thing that extinguishes fire; but perhaps a fire, by the side of which the sun is black—or a light the opposite of our daylight, by the side of which the night and the day are alike—in which worlds float like specks, or as animalculæ in water. We call good a principle, when it is only *our way of estimating the phenomena* of life. Think you there is any good where there is no sense to feel? So good and evil, being only *our* estimate, must belong *to us*—and *we* are the principle after all. We judge by reason of sense. Then may not sense be that formless, unchangeable, infinite something that is not a thing—that hidden and undefinable fire whose sparks are our thoughts, and whose warmth is our life? A fire, whose quenching by the INFINITE WILL gives forms of matter in the cooling—to be fanned into a blaze by a breath of HIS LIFE—things all luminous within, darkened outwardly as if by a contraction of the sense? May not sense be the INFINITE SUBSTANCE of all space? in which thought is as the rolling of worlds, and it, pulsating with motions and emotions, whispers and voices that do not strike upon our dull senses—so stupid are we. Even our atmosphere pulsates as a breath, and the ether vibrates to every voice or thought, and the "aching void" far beyond all suns, worlds and universes—that void of nothingness where GOD is enthroned as "THE OVER-SOUL" of all—even there the tremblings of thought and feeling meet an answering response! What *do* we know after all? We know this: It is SENSE that is trying to define itself in this contradictory manner we call nature. Out of it and into it come so-called principles, laws and things—as the breath going out and coming in. It is the actor, the cause, the source of a mighty river called life.

There are other senses of which we have never dreamed—as the unknown is beyond the known. How small and weak is the latter compared to the former! How small the possible in comparison to the impossible! Is the SUPERNATURAL the IMPOSSIBLE? Then how great and vast it must be! It is natural to grow in knowledge, but the things unknown are infinite—*they are all in our ignorance.* How vast it is compared to our knowledge! Is IGNORANCE the SUPERNATURAL? The light that flows from the sun is small compared to the limitless *darkness* that hovers around its radius. Is the DARKNESS the SUPERNATURAL? The above is greater than the below. Is it to be wondered at that men have universally looked *up* to GOD? However vast nature may be there is something still above it, which, although incomprehensible, still has an existence to every thinking mind. My nature is limited by my knowledge of myself and my relationship to others. So nature is a limited thing. as my mind is my limit. May not this nature, after all, be merely a *mental product,* as the good and evil of it is? A mental product ! not of one, or even of a race, but of all minds in unison ! Is all nature outside of us, or is it *within*, as a wondrous mystery hidden in our ignorance.

Is not the impossible *within us*, the same as weakness, and ignorance, and darkness?

Education is nothing but the opening of a " door," or the lighting of a lamp in a dark place, through which things before unknown appear to us as the possible, and are very simple. The circumstances of our lives are all within us, as the possibilities of our natures, but hidden from us in our *ignorance*, till our acts flow out as a light, showing us merely a *few* things of the many still lying back in the infinite darkness of the unexplored beyond. The hidden is infinite. We are hidden from ourselves, and know not the wondrous powers lying back of our smallness. Even we are astonished at the wondrous skill of this thing we call man, which is but the supernatural revealing itself to us. It is very close to us— possibly it may be us! hidden from us, as all things are hidden from the infant's closed eyes. I feel so, at least at times, when I forget the narrow limits of this life, and it is my effort herein to show what acts are the greatest lights in this infinite darkness of ignorance, so that peradventure some one more gifted than I, may possibly surprise the Supernatural himself some day with the torch, lighted not by man.

It may be an idle task to search for GOD, but he has given us questioning minds, and every instinct of nature prompts us to ask, " Who and what is GOD?" and I realize that the world grows by each apparent or pretended solution of it. Possibly GOD joins himself to us in this way from out the shoreless darkness of our own natures.

The first letters of GOD's alphabet is nature. They are multitudinous—for each object is a letter. What is the word? "The word of GOD" is the sense of all these things when reduced back from the contradictions of multiplicity to one. It then becomes intelligible to sense of a limited capacity. For nothing less than infinity can comprehend the meaning of all things. But the sense of the finite mind is the same as that of the infinite mind. All things are in ONE, and exist *in it* and *of it*, but not FROM it.

In this infinite variety of things—this multiplicity of objects—this division of the one—the mind goes back in search of the first principle, the foundation from which they all spring. This infinite principle of power is sense. The vast oceans of space pulsate with sense. The worlds, suns, stars and objects of space are each and all held together and kept in place by sense. All things are suspended in an ocean of sense. Nay! things *are sense*— and sensible, if the darkness would roll from off our souls. Sense is the only thing in existence that comprehends things. To comprehend is to enclose, or envelop. God reveals himself to the sense of things. In fact, he is sense itself.

God exists not as an objective, but as a subjective being —not separate and apart from nature, but as the creative principle thereof, residing in all and permeating all that is. In this view the supernatural becomes comprehensible.   It is the soul of nature and objects: hence GOD is objectified in his works.   He who looks for GOD as an object to worship will find many on the road to power, but he who looks for GOD *within himself* will feel the fullness of satisfaction and power, which GOD gives to all who love the good and true.   That which is unchangeable is supernatural and eternal.   In nature things are mutable.   Matter may be divided till there is nothing left of it.   Analyze a thing, and you have nothing left of it save a little dross.   Take a chair for example.   What is it?   A few pieces of wood put together for use.   Take it to pieces and the chair vanishes.   Burn the wood and we have ashes.   Melt the ashes and we have some other substances to which science gives names.   But where and what is the chair?   Is it a mere name? or is it a substance?   It is an effect—a result of the combination of pieces of wood.   If it is an effect, where and what is the cause?   I answer, the chair was first an *idea conceived in the mind of some man*, and came *out* of the man, and was formed in matter for use.   But the real chair is an idea, and hence it is as indestructible as man himself. The same is true of all things that man makes.   They come out of man as the light of his *intelligence* illuminates the darkness of his *ignorance*, wherein infinity exists. Nature is matter, motion and space, but the sense of it is the supernatural.   It interprets itself, as I am feebly trying to do.   Each man must interpret for himself, and his interpretation will be *himself* merely, as the sense of his mind illumines the darkness within.   Space is a vacuum in which things exist *in motion,* or in *sense.*   It is the "OVER-SOUL," and *comprehends* or includes all. This is the supernatural. The sense of a thing gives it motion, and in motion things gestate, as in a womb, and grow, or become materialized.

At the centre of things there are no things, neither is there any motion there. Perfection and stagnation exist at the centre. The centre is a vacuum, and is *the* soul.

All worlds wheel around centres, and centres are souls, and souls are GODS. In GOD ("The Over-Soul") all things are possible—in nature, where soul is a centre, the impossible exists, because here is ignorance, darkness and weakness. "He who limits things by his narrow sense is a fool," says HARGRAVE JENNINGS, one of England's great Rosicrucians; and I say, whoever limits the possible shows his weakness and want of comprehension. We do not know what exists in nature. We know very little, and what little we know is a damage to us, save as it shows us our weakness and the power and infinitude of the possible. To return to ideas.

We are as we think : ideas rule and govern all action and all growth. Ideas are souls—entities of all being—unchangeable and indestructible; they exist in the spirit ; the atmosphere is the spirit of the earth, and in it are the souls of vegetation having been evolved from the earth. They hover around, and when conditions are favorable they descend according to the law of attraction and affinity, and spring up in the soil of vegetation. Vegetation does not depend altogether upon seeds, it springs spontaneously from the earth. To illustrate : when a young man, my father burned several coal pits on one bed during the winter; the next fall, in passing by, I saw several plants, commonly called the *Mullen*, growing in the old coal bed. The *Mullen plant was unknown* in that part of the country previously. A man in Northern Iowa dug a well over one hundred feet in depth. The great pile of clay lay there in the sunlight and darkness, wept over by dew and rain, scorched in summer and froze in winter, till the next year it produced a crop of weeds that were not to be found anywhere in all the country round about.

It is a well known fact to the pioneers of the wilderness of northern Pennsylvania (and, I suppose to, other woodlands) that on a newly cleared piece of woodland when the soil is killed by burning, "fire-weeds" spring up almost as thick as the hair on an animal's back.

There is such a thing as chemical affinity; and the earth being prepared by heat or in any other manner makes "conditions" for new or old forms of vegetation to come into existence. The earth's atmosphere is all alive with ideas—ideas of vegetables, animals and men— all waiting for favorable conditions to enable them to be born into existence. Ideas are infinite in number and variety, corresponding to all conditions from mineral up to man. They are the soul-life and volition of matter, and they enter into matter at every point where conditions are favorable. A scientist told me the other day that a drop of nitric acid applied to a piece of fresh broken granite rock, revealed under the microscope numerous living beings similar to animalculæ found in stagnant water. "This," said he, "proves that the solid rock is full of life." But it proves no such thing. It simply shows that the union of the acid with the rock produced motion there, and wherever there is motion there is a magnetic current, and forms having life spring into existence—not that they were any more in the rock than in the acid, or that of necessity they were in either. I hold that all forms are ideas materialized, that ideas are eternal, but forms are evanescent. The sunlight gives color to vegetation ; color is an idea, but, although the foundation of color may reside in the mineral of plants, yet we all know that the sun develops it. A child develops in utero, but who does not know that the soul comes through the father? Matter is the mother ; spirit is the father.

In every atom of matter is a vacuum—else there would be no attraction—for matter crowds upon vacuum and hence takes form, and vacuum is the womb of matter, into which ideas are attracted whenever moved by a magnetic current.

All life and organization are dependent upon this current, and this is dependent upon the formation of a magnet, or the union of the positive and negative, the acid and alkali, the father and mother. As spirit is the father, and as ideas (souls) come from the Father, so does spirit baptize matter, impregnating it. "God is a spirit." So the supernatural is a spirit, and will beget itself in matter whenever conditions are favorable. It is upon exactly the same principle as the generation of mosquitoes in stagnant water. Low weak forms are generated in low conditions. Ideas, being soul, are food for souls. Hence man grows in creative and *original* power through his reception of ideas. Ideas take root in the soil of man's mind *according to its condition*, exactly as vegetation springs up in the soil of the earth. If the soil be poor the vegetation will be inferior If the mind be low and vulgar, tne ideas attracted will be inferior ; but ideas of whatever grade or kind are a creative power, There is a spontaneity of mind as well as of earth. That which springs up of itself is generally weeds, but the most delicious fruits are produced by effort—culture. The higher the culture, the nearer the approximation to the supernatural. To show the road thereto is my object.

Look you at the burrowing worm, and at the soaring eagle ! Step up, slowly, laboriously, from the lowest form, step by step, to the highest form of life known on this planet—man. Do you stop here ? And because your poor sight sees no higher form will you deny its existence ? Do you see intelligence graded from the snail to the loftiest . intellect, and then, by your narrow sense, limit grada-tion of power ? Behold the grass of the fields ! the lilies of the valley ! Then look aloft, by day or by night, at the wondrous manifestation of an intelligent power, and blush in shame at your presumption.

We grasp a little of knowledge, a little of life, a little of spirit by the five senses, but the vital principles of science and of human action are only grasped by the loftiest reason. This is intuition. Are you a reasonable being, and yet limit GOD by denying him ? If so, your reason is of the lowest order ; it is destructive ; it is not GOD-like and creative. Analyze matter in the crucible of thought—dissect all forms with the scalpel of reason, and then when you are done with your work tell me what you know. If your work has not inspired you with a love of the unknown mystery surrounding and dwelling within all things, you are an egotist. If you cavil at names you are a fool. Are you an artist? Then take your inspirations from one who works eternally, and never makes a failure. Are you a mechanic? Go study the suspension bridges the spider makes, and the comb of the honey bee, or the mechanism of a tree. I need not multiply words. Whatever you are, or whatever you aspire to be, the power is waiting for you—the paterns are spread out for your study.

The supernatural is in all, and is subservient to our wishes. But it is our work to make conditions—these have no limit. There is no interference—you can be just what you like to be; but growth is slow. Why hurry? Is not eternity for us? It is the hurry and worry of life that destroys power. Trouble and vexation destroy health and pleasure, and these are all there is of value. All things are suggestive, for they are ideas; they call us out of ourselves to revel in the infinite. Is there no suggestion that comes to you, kind reader, of the supernatural? Is there no intuitive feeling that speaks to you of immortal, undying power? Do you not, in your better moods, long to drink at the fountain of life, pleasure and individuality? If not, I am sorry for you. Ideas give fulness of life and pleasure—the greater the idea, the greater fulness and power. What idea is greater than the supernatural?

We talk glibly of the laws of nature, as if they were fixed and immutable ; but they are set aside by every habit which disgraces the race. Furthermore, modern times are rife with accounts of the dead appearing to the living, and of the living appearing as the dead : of levitation and the moving of substance without a motive power, etc., etc. The suspension of any one law of nature proves beyond all question that all are subject to the same power, and all *may* be suspended or rendered inoperative.

II. PRINCIPLES OF NATURE.

I believe in definitions; but all definition is arbitrary. To define a thing is a creation. That nature exists is a certainty, but when we come to define it we shall find it not so simple. We define things in order that we may understand each other.

We speak of nature as if it was an entity—an individual thing. But the fact is, there are myriads of things and conditions in nature which are parts thereof. In all this diversity, there must be a something the intellect can seize upon as a *fact* upon which to stand while we search in this whirl of atoms and worlds for a stationary principle of being. To find that, which is common to all, is to find the real. If nature is divided into parts, it exists as a whole; every part must have something common to the whole.

To analyze a part, is to analyze the whole, for the same laws inhere in an atom, as in a world. An atom exists by the same laws that the earth does; and its modes of action are the same. The law whereby matter coheres and gathers together, is attraction. This is a binding force. But the law that dissolves atoms, and throws them off, is the law of repulsion. These two—the positive and the negative—constitute the laws of motion. Everything exists by virtue of motion; but there is a point where there is no motion. That point is the centre from whence motion takes its rise. At the centre of the earth there is no up nor down, no positive nor negative; it is simply vacant of these things—*i. e.* all things exist here in solution, as it were—or conditionless.

Things differ in nature. Shall we say, then, that nature does not exist because there are so many natures? By no means: for there are two laws, acting in all conditions, which belong to that *real nature*, which is the substratum. They flow out from it as the positive and negative flows from a magnet. As there is a neutral point between the positive and negative, a point where neither exists; so nature is a neutral ground. lying between antagonistic forces.

Nature may be likened unto a magnet; which, in itself, moves not, but sends out positive and negative forces. To a thing belongs motion and space; without motion nothing could exist. It is motion that fills the void, and prevents *nothing* from asserting its sway. *Things* in *motion* must have *space* to move in; so all things are triune in manifestation. A thing is composed of two visible and one invisible points; one visible point is space in which it exists; the other is the thing itself; but the third, or invisible point is its motion. The earth and space surrounding it are visible, but its motions are invisible. It stands still, and we are always on the top. The soul of nature is motion, or rather, that which produces motion. Hence, the third part of things, which is the most important part, is invisible. Matter, space and sense are the three things which constitute nature. Matter needs no definition. Space is known, and is relatively a vacuum; but the sense thereof is known not by visibility. The relative proves the absolute, the same as a part proves the whole. A relative vacuum proves an absolute vacuum; as relative sense proves an absolute sense. Existence is that which is visible, or that which comes *en raport* with visible things. The invisible and the unknown are the absolute. The nearer we approach the unknown the more we are entering the realm of power, and losing our hold on visible and tangible things. The nature of a thing is its conditions, and these conditions are only its mode of action. As there are only two laws of action—if those laws are followed to their source we shall find nature herself totally *stagnant* and *indifferent*.

I am aware there is a class of thinkers who claim that there is no inertia, and that "nature abhors a vacuum." This may be true, but it is far, *very far*, from evident. It is just as logical to claim that nature is "one vast whole," and that it is *not* made up of parts or conditions. I claim, that inertia is a condition in which no motion or life is visible, or that is known; and this is the *dividing line* between the two great contending powers, attraction and repulsion. Furthermore, I claim that a vacuum exists in matter—the source of its attractive and repulsive power, and that said vacuum is foreign to nature, *i.e.* a prisoner in conditions. Its efforts to free itself give rise to motions, analagous to combustion. This is, indeed, the soul of things.

That nature is a relentless, unfeeling, remorseless power, needs no argument. It moves on, regardless of the waste of worlds, or the sacrifice of life or forms. To nature, death is the same as birth and life, as if it were a stranger.

Nature suffers not; neither does she enjoy. Remove sensation from nature and it is neither good nor evil. The earth, water, air, electricity, the sun, moon and stars, without something to make comparisons, are all indifferently good or evil alike. There can be no good or evil save to things that suffer and enjoy. This indifference corresponds to ignorance, for out of indifferent nature comes all of life, even as knowledge springs from ignorance. Absolutely nature exists only as *sense*, in which view we are nothing, and matter is nothing; but we, as relative beings, know literally nothing of the absolute. Hence, the folly of reasoning from an absolute standpoint.

It is claimed, that evolution is *the* law of nature. This is partly true, for evolution is due to repulsion. Repulsion is the first law of existence, and is the male principle, from which sprung the female principle—attraction. (See the allegory of Adam's rib.) All motion is circular; and matter thrown from a centre must return in time. There are no straight lines in existence. The returning current of a magnet is negative, or female.

Revolution is the law of nature, inasmuch as it includes both repulsion and attraction. A circle is symbolic of eternity. The soul, in its efforts to free itself from conditions, projects a magnetic stream from itself, which describes a circle in its motion. As magnetism (or, more properly, spirit) moves in chaos—that part of the current which is negative or female—polarizes or combines matter from chaos—and thus peoples space with stars or worlds. The negative is the combining current. It is formative. The earth upon the same principle evolves spirit from itself, *i. e.*, dissolves and throws off matter in a refined state, which in its return deposits the germs of vegetation, animals or man, upon and in the earth's surface, impregnating it, and they grow. Growth is motion —or evolution of spirit, and involution of matter from the unknown, chaotic state, combining into forms. Growth is only matter in motion, according to the laws of motion, which are circular or revolutional. Evolution!! Indeed ! It is not half of the truth. What of involution? Like the light from a candle, refined matter is being evolved from matter, which radiates round about, and as constantly returns, bringing from the unknown something of the infinite to combine in forms of beauty and use. Transient and fleeting as these forms may be, they each and all contain souls struggling for freedom, and the ocean from whence they came ; the stream of life, flows downward, and not upward. God is above—but things being less are beneath. Causation is hidden in the bosom of mystery and the darkness of the impenetrable shadow; but effects follow the light, and flow on ever as worlds, suns, stars, and human beings.

All matter, all life, all forms, and all mind is involved in an unfathomable mystery, which enters into existence in the light, taking form as matter and thought. If this were not so, matter would become less and less by its action; for light is but the consumption of matter. The evolution of matter is the *involution* of GOD, which increases as light increases.

But oh! the mystery of the night surrounding us! Who can fathom its depths? Who can explore infinitude? Things reside in the shadow from which they come stealthily into the light for a little time—then steal away into the shadow again. Man with his torch gropes his way slowly and with cautious steps in the thick darkness, and anon some grotesque shape comes partially in view —then disappears as if the light had dissolved it. The darkness, rendered more intense by the presence of light, crowds around before and behind; and upon the confines of light—in the twilight of being—the formless takes form, and such as can bear the light march in serried columns along with man.

The light we carry is what we have learned. It enables us to see and define that which otherwise were formless.

WHAT IS LIFE?

To define, life is to live: for in our efforts to define a thing or principle, we unconsciously become like that which we attack. Analysis without definition is destruction. To define life is a herculean task. Life is a manifestation of something having power to feel which resides in an organization. All things visible are simply effects of some hidden cause—causes are always hidden. The true mode of reasoning is from effects towards causes, which, receding as we advance, we only approximate. Life, as we understand it, is a result of the union of soul and spirit. It is impossible to tell *what* a thing is; any word or name that expresses what we mean is the best we can do. The Word of GOD is the meaning of GOD; and the word of LIFE is the significance thereof, which is the object of this book. It is the desire of every earnest person to know why we are here; and in order to answer the question, it is better to explain modes of action than to multiply names. I look upon life as matter and sense in union or in motion : for all motion is the cause of union of atoms. As I have said before, motion is the soul or sense of things. The laws of motion are the laws of combustion, for they are the same. Everything reminds us of the fire out of which we came, and to which all things return in the last analysis.

To find a something common to all forms of matter—animate and inanimate—is to find that real nature I am trying to define; that will be a fact as real as existence itself; *that fact is that which we feel and know.* In other words, that perception of life which comes through the five senses, and not through that higher or intellectual sense.

By virtue of these five senses the earth appears as an undulating plain, with the sun rising, moving over head, and setting at night. We are always on the top of the earth, and the heavens are above.

No mode of reasoning can make us *feel* that we are half of the time underneath—or standing out sideways in space. That this is owing to our relationship to the earth I freely admit, but the knowledge we have gained through the exercise of the higher intellect sets aside the basic facts of existence, and proves them a delusion of sense. Now which is correct? May not the facts of intellect be a delusion of sense, also? There is no absoluteness in man, save his existence.

These same senses cause us to feel pleasure and pain. Are they real? or is it a delusion of sense? These senses tell us of the up and the down, and the reversal of ourselves is death. We instinctively love pleasure, which we call GOOD, and elevate it as GOD. But we dread pain, and avoid it as the devil, which is low down and to be kept down, if possible. Reason as you will, sail around the globe, explore space and measure the stars, and then teach that there is no high and no low, no good nor evil, no up nor down ; but still *common sense* remains —as nature remains—a solemn protest against the light of the intellect as a guide to those deep and fundamental principles of existence; which to be of any value must bring pleasure instead of pain. Human reason leads the soul to nothing; while the universal instinct warns man of the evils of pain and death,—as if creative genius has planted in man a something in which the brute shares —that causes him to dread death, and to value life. And furthermore an instinct that tells him of a nature long since forgotten, save in legend; of the unnatural state in which he now lives, or rather suffers, and of a supernatural state to which he may attain.

The common sense of atoms teaches them to lie still in their places in obedience to attraction, and the same teaches them to fly when set free by repulsion. The same laws make all things related, and all life one homogeneous whole. We are relative beings, and as such, logic, to be of any use, must be relative also. Common sense corresponds to indifference or to inertia, because it is ignorance. But what is the knowledge worth which destroys common sense and the naturalness of things? That which destroys nature, destroys happiness.

Who so bold as to assert that the wisdom of man adds to his happiness? The first manifestation of nature is law or action, which is two-fold, as I have stated. This must be nature, which, as a cause, is superior to effects, as an artist is superior to his works. Man, as an effect of nature, is inferior, but GOD, who is the Author of nature, is superior to all. Nature cannot be infinite, for it is particled, and is bounded and limited as a whole. There can be only one thing in existence as an absolute entity. The word is superior to the letters composing it, but the sense is superior to both. Thoughts are letters of an unknown alphabet, nature is the word, GOD is the sense. That which destroys the word takes away the sense. The thought of the age is that there is no GOD; such is the unnaturalness of man. The life-principle is one homogeneous whole; it cannot be particled; it is the same in worm as in man. The little life of one thing is just as potent, and as great *for that thing*, as the greater life is for another. If the life of one thing is immortal, then all life is. But the life may be beaten out of a thing by processes, to be explained hereafter, so that it, as a thing, has no self-supporting power.

Everything is dual—"Male and female created he them,"—darkness and light, ignorance and intelligence, cold and heat, evil and good, opposites, antagonists, all go hand in hand—inseparable. There is nothing known but has its opposite; and one being given, the other may be found close at hand. Furthermore, the third thing, that which makes the triangle of imperfection, resides always within the two visible parts. Two things being placed side by side are said to be in contact; but there is always *something between* them, which prevents them from becoming one, for absolute contact is oneness. That which separates things is condition. Distance is condition. If all things were in like condition, they would fuse and blend so that all form would be lost. This third thing—that is not a thing—this something intangible and immaterial, I call the soul of things; for by virtue of it things exist and have motion. Distance is space, and space is a vacuum. Hence all forms have souls, for there is a condition or distance between all forms. That which is visible and tangible has its antagonist or opposite. Its *antagonist is that which destroys* it, and not that which sustains it. Indifferent nature is antagonized by life. All life which has volition preys upon and sustains itself by that which has no volition. This is very evident in herbivorous animals, but not quite so evident in the carnivora; though when we stop to consider that the flesh of the sheep is due to vegetation, upon which it lives, it becomes evident how the wolf feeds upon vegetation which has gone through a chemical change in the form of the sheep. After death all things are indifferent. Flesh is as indifferent after death as vegetation. Nature, then, being visible, has its visible antagonist. The antagonist of nature being life, the highest type of life calls for our attention: that is, man.

III. THE UNNATURAL.

What is man ? He is the highest form known, containing in himself the greatest quantity of life, the most
intelligence, the greatest will, the most creative power.
Indifferent nature corresponds to darkness, ignorance,
weakness, want of power. The ancient philosophers called
the earth "the egg of the night." Out of darkness all
things come. Ignorance is the mother of all conditions;
in ignorance we begin this life, and struggle towards the
light of intelligence; from the miasmatic swamps of
ignorance come all conditions that we war against. A
certain form contains a certain amount of life, and
wherever there is conscious life there is pain and pleasure. Life gives pleasure, but its deficiency causes pain.
To increase life is the road to pleasure; the deficiency
of life causes the *unnatural* to appear, viz: pain.
Indifferent nature is as full of life as it will contain, and
we have no reason to suppose that there is pain or
pleasure therein. But to me nature seems in an ecstacy
of growth and decay, and that man, by violation of
laws, has fallen beneath the *floor ecstatic*, into an ocean
of tears, whose waves alternately howl with storms of
agony, or sing with zephyrs of melodious pleasure.

But the moment consciousness came into existence,
coupled with will and power to act, having volition as

freedom of action, that moment commenced the creation of conditions altogether different than had previously existed. I care nothow slow the process,—it takes ages to produce some things. Every worm that burrows in the earth, everything that crawls upon its surface, every bird that plucks a seed or eats a worm, every animal that crops the herbage of the plains, or that devours other animals, up to man, who tunnels the earth, plows the ground, or improves vegetation, fruits and animals; he who scans the heavens, fathoms and bridges the cceans, and subdues and subjugates all other things, these are all creators—creators of conditions : conditions wherein there is less of harmony, less of fulness of life. The action of will is exhaustive, especially its *over-action*, which comes from ignorance of the laws of action. . In our ignorance of the future we get an imaginative idea of some great good, to be derived from doing some certain thing. Immediately we set about it, and, being led captive by the object in view, regardless of heat and cold, hunger or thirst, pain or pleasure, we rush along till exhausted. Exhaustion is disease. IT IS UNNATURAL ! All disease is unnatural. It comes from action !—the action of a FREE WILL. That man should be the most unnatural being in existence, comes not only from his freedom of action, but from his greater range of action, his greater power of thought, invention, and imagination. If nature be considered indifferent, man antagonizes it in every particular. He is a being of thought, judgment, memory, imagination, craft, love, and will. Pride and ambition are his ruling traits. Many there be who claim that all things are natural; that there is no above or below nature; that man cannot violate or go contrary to nature's laws. The inevitable conclusion derived from the foregoing is, that man is a mere machine, moving only as he is moved upon. That there is no such thing as volition: no high, no low, no merit or demerit, no good, no evil. Any man with common sense knows such conclusions to be false. Why? Because it is contrary to experience, and every-day *facts* of existence. By virtue of our organization, by virtue of the conditions of our very existence, there exists the up and down, the high and low, etc., and any conclusions of logic, which set these mundane facts aside, are based on false premises.

What a demon nature or GOD must be, to hold us responsible for the violation of laws, when we have no power to help ourselves. But, they assert further, that there is no violation of law ; that nature's laws *cannot* be broken. I simply say, Gentlemen, you know better ; anyone of common sense can see the absurdity of such ideas. Do we not suffer for the violence we do to ourselves ? Most assuredly. Then why does nature, or GOD, NECESSITY, or FATE make us suffer for doing that which we cannot help doing ? Man is of necessity a law maker, and, in his ignorance, *cannot conform* to nature's laws. To conform to nature would be to revolve in an eternal circle; but man, in striving for the new, breaks through the circle of ignorance and indifference, and gets hurt in so doing. Thus he becomes diseased by his own act. I freely admit that he cannot help violating the law on account of ignorance, but each act or violation is a *creation*, and is more pleasing to man because it is his own. And furthermore, the ignorance we complain of is *in ourselves*, and not in surroundings. Thus we compel ourselves to act; each act creates light, and light is the object of our existence. Evil is our teacher. It is wisely ordered that we shonld suffer; for that increases action or light, to which we are responsible, and by which all are judged. We are nature, necessity, or fate.

"Whatever is, is right!" No, indeed: the reverse is nearer the truth. There is nothing true to its condition; if things were true and right, there would be no need of improvement, and no possible room for it. There would be no foreshadowing of a better state of things: no aspirations, no longings, no heart aches, nor weariness of soul. There is little of right and truth in all things; just enough to give us a taste of the good, and make us dissatisfied with our present condition, and spur us on to effort to better it. No man can climb who is at the top of the ladder. Truth and right are far, very far, above us, but we get flashes and gleams of the glory occasionally, which shows us where we stand on the ladder. Hideous, weird, fantastic shapes glare out of the darkness beneath, but above us is light, truth, knowledge, love, glory, harmony. Nature is harmony, but the unnatural is discord. Man is unnatural because he is *less* than nature. He pretends to love nature, but in reality he despises it. We are creatures of art. We are made up mainly of hereditary and acquired habits. These have become a second nature, which we admire. This second nature I call the unnatural. True, nature keeps along with us in our downward course, and fights manfully against disease ; restoring us in sleep, and adapting itself to our vices and crimes. It is our *voluntary* powers which ruin us, but it is the *involuntary* which gives us what little health we have. When we forget ourselves in sweet sleep, nature asserts itself; and even then the abnormal habits of our daily lives prevents her work. There is very little *indifferent* sleep. We are too intense; the intensity of the day disturbs the night. We cannot forget that which we love : our daily avocations, our graspings, our hoarding up, our over-reaching of each other : these haunt us in our sleep. Nature must play second. Our natural habits we are ashamed of, and hide them away as we cover our nakedness. We take no lesson even from innocent childhood —glimpses of the kingdom of glory—but our earliest recollections are pointings of the finger of shame.

To be dignified is the glory of civilization. To suppress natural laughter, and smile instead, is grand ; to " put the best side out," and to conceal the natural ; to pretend to be greater, or better than we are ; to think more of our looks, walk, manners, clothing, and the wealth we have robbed the poor of—this is civilization. To turn away from one poorly clad, not deigning an answer to a civil question ; to look coldly in the eye of a stranger, without speaking when accosted, because

you have not been introduced: this is dignity; this is
fashionable. To bow down to kings, Popes, priests, and
the nobility ; to shout and hurrah when they show themselves ; to toil to support them in their pomp and
idleness ; to march in serried columns to deadly strife with
each other; to murder each other without enmity—
this it is to be civilized. The earth is drenched with
human gore, and her fair fields are rich with the bone-
dust of humanity. The glory of one nation is the destruction of another. What for? To perpetuate the dam-
nable and unnatural idea that some men are better than
others; that some were made to rule while others were
made to serve. Man has made this earth one vast pande-
monium—a cesspool, out of which come malarial vapors
and malarial beings, distorted in body, deformed in
mind, dwarfed in spirit.

Look at the diabolical crimes—the fiendish actions of
men, the wrong and outrage—at the deadly diseases constantly on the increase in type and malignancy—and
then say, if you can, that these things are natural. I cannot. Alas ! how we degrade nature or GOD in the bare
idea. Not willing to assume the responsibility that
nature puts upon him, he, ADAM-like, hides behind the
fig leaves his nakedness, and ascribes to fate, nature,
chance or necessity the actions he is ashamed of. " Forced
into the world, forced through it, and forced out again,"
he thinks force will bear the blame, suffer the penalty,
and take all the responsibility of his actions ; while at
the same time he is groaning under adversity, and suffer-

ing from disease resulting from his own acts, which he might have avoided with a little knowledge and self-control.

The natural and the unnatural go hand in hand, as matter and sense, body and mind, the voluntary and involuntary, ignorance and knowledge—the same as the opposite poles of a magnet. The moment the two poles *unite*, there is no longer a current—the poles cease to exist. But so long as the poles are separated, or connected by matter in a *different condition*, the magnetic current, like a stream, passes from the positive to the negative. But unite the poles so that there shall be no opposing conditions between them, and the magnet ceases to be a magnet. The telegraphic wire, making the circuit of the earth, or a portion of it, carries messages back and forth, but it emits sparks, and leaves its messages only where the line is *disconnected*. If you say the *current exists*, although not visible, when the connection is perfect, you assert that which cannot be demonstrated. The two poles of a battery being connected by a wire, no current is perceptible, and I have no way of knowing of a current only as I form a part of the circuit with my body. I then feel the current passing through my nerves. This feeling is produced by the resistance of my nerves. The matter of which my body is composed is not in the same condition as the matter composing the wires, and, although both may be good conductors, yet these conditions of matter serve the same purpose as a disconnection of the poles ; and there where the obstacle is, the force is patent.

Matter and sense (or mind) are the two poles of an invisible magnet. Sense is no more a result of matter than matter is a result of sense. They both exist, and are mutually dependent, not upon each other, but upon the magnet. In the magnet we glimpse the SUPERNATURAL in the MAGIC MIRROR—NATURE, INERTIA, INDIFFERENCE, as an IMAGE of the real reversed.

IV.—BODY AND SPIRIT.

Man is the ultimate, or fruit of the tree of life. The lower orders of aminate creatures may be termed the roots, trunk, branches, leaves, etc.,—but man is the fruit. Some say "he is an epitome of the Universe." This is a mistaken idea. Men differ one from another as the lower animals differ, or the various orders of vegetables. The apple is a species of fruit, but there are many *varieties* of apples. However much men differ in looks, form, manners and disposition, there is one peculiarity notice-able in all, viz: the correspondence to the lower orders. We all resemble, more or less, some variety of the lower orders; and the less the resemblance the further is the removal therefrom. Some have the tiger, lion, vulture, hawk, eagle, sheep, goat, cat, lynx, ox, owl, ser-pent, various kinds of fishes, etc., etc., "*ad infinitum*," predominating. Some by their build and motions show that they have just come up out of the water—or, possibly, may be going back into it. Man is an epitome of the *elements he has developed up through.* We carry something of what we have been along with us—viz: the spirit.

And some men, having developed up through certain elements, are an *epitome of those* elements, but not of others. Elements are infinite; but power is not based in elements, neither can immortality be predicated therein.

Animals are but vegetables cut loose at the roots ; man differs from them only in degree. He has all that they have, and a little more, generally, in some directions ; but some animals are nearer human than some men. According to DARWIN, man has descended from the ape. According to my notion, there is as much logic in saying that the ape is a degenerated man. "It is a poor rule that won't work both ways." If a man ascends he also descends. We make distinctions, in our ignorance of principles, which, in reality, do not exist. If an animal can develop into a man, a man may go down to an animal. Progression is no more a law than retrogression. If man ever had a beginning, he certainly must have an end, no matter how long it may be delayed. If he progress eternally, he certainly cannot always remain man. Progress means change, growth to better conditions, *and conditions change the form* and nature. If man never had a beginning, he can never have an end. But, suppose this idea to be true, and progression without retrogression to be the law of being, is it not a little strange that man is no higher in the scale of being after having been eternally progressing? Remember, the eternity of the past is the same as that of the future. Why is he no greater if he has always existed and been always growing? If he is merely an infant on this earth, is it logical to conclude that he will remain the same and still keep on growing eternally? The distinctions we make between things are merely arbitrary. Life is one. Man has no more right to immortality than the brute. Man, in his

pride and egotism, claims for himself a special creation
and existence after death, but denies it to the brute. This
is not a logical deduction. Man is a name merely
that we give to a manifestation of life to distinguish it
from other manifestations. We make distinctions to
which we give names, which are very satisfactory to
most men. Like the Arkansas man, who, when accosted
by a traveler, asking information about his way, instead
of giving the information desired, cocked his hat over
one eye, struck an attitude, and asked the traveler, "What
mought your name be, sir?" Names are very satisfactory to children, but he who seeks for principles, cares
little for names. But in order to convey ideas, and to
be understood, and to distinguish one thing from another,
names are important. "Man," then, is the name given
to the highest type of life we are acquainted with on
this earth, and the term body is applied to the visible
part. But the real man is an idea—as much so as that
represented by any piece of mechanism. (See deffini-
tions of ideas in previous parts of this work.) In order
to a more perfect understanding of man and his powers,
we will divide him into parts—but the distinctions herein
made are arbitrary, and do not really exist. Man is composed of body, mind, spirit, and soul ; or in other words,
the ego, the thought, and the thing thought of—or
power, motion, and the thing moved. But these things
are an unity. There can be only one *principle* in existence.
The moment you admit two, one bounds and limits the
other. Very suggestive of the positive and negative
poles of a magnet. Laying all speculation aside, we do

not know what " infinity " is, more than we know what man or anything else is. If we should, at some time, discover what it is, it would, after all, be only another *name* added to our vocabulary. I cannot find a name for " *her who is nameless,*" that third thing—the MOTHER of POWER and WEAKNESS—of GOD and of nature. The loftiest thought cannot go beyond the realm of things— for thought belongs to things. The most fertile imagination cannot find a field that does not exist, in which to revel.

The insane is as real as the sane, although *we* may not think it desirable or healthy. Perhaps there are some who love insanity. Who shall say that the dividing line between sanity and insanity is a fiction? That dividing line—that neutral ground—is the body,—matter.

Science is unable to tell us of *all* the substances that compose the human form. There is something which escapes the closest analysis, or the most subtile and searching thought. The scalpel fails to find the spirit— so science fails to find aught but the dross of these bodies. There is a something hidden away in matter that holds each atom in its place—aye! and gives form to all atoms—which is master, and yet a prisoner : lord, but yet a servant. There is a something in matter lying latent, which is not heat nor flame, but which, when let loose, produces heat, flame and combustion. It is the "Fire" the ancient Magi worshipped. It is not magnetism, nor the astral fluid, neither is it light, nor electricity; for these are but *effects* of its freedom. There is a spark lying dormant in matter, which, when aroused by friction, decomposes all forms. If set in motion gently and by degrees, it refines matter and causes growth, attracting and repelling matter. If struck out by violence, it produces conflagrations and destruction. Worlds are sustained and destroyed by this spark of fire. It is a useful servant to man, but when it gets beyond his control it is a cruel and remorseless master. THIS FIRE IS THE SPIRIT. It is in all things, and is the life thereof. In fact, things are but forms of spirit condensed. Life is a liberation of spirit. All matter evolves from itself an aura, peculiar to its condition. This aura is produced by the gentle motion of things, in growth and in death. All atoms are in motion, for spirit is ceaselessly active. Swedenborg says there is a *sphere* belonging to and surrounding all things. It is more perceptible in some things than in others. Baron Reichenbach instituted a series of experiments with various metals and stones which he submitted to sensitive persons in a darkened chamber, and has written a work in which he claims the same thing as true, so far as tested by him. This aura I term spirit, or a result of the action of that hidden fire, which has been worshipped in ancient days as GOD, in honor of which the eternal altar-fires were kept burning, and men bowed down to the sun and worshipped Him as the most perfect symbol of fire, or GOD. All matter is undergoing change, and this change is growth, and growth is life, and life is the freeing of fire or spirit. All matter is in a state of combustion; some forms slowly, others with great intensity. This combustion may not be perceptible to our dull

senses, but that only proves our blindness. Growth is
the throwing off effete matter and taking on new.
This is exactly the case with violent combustion. A
burning pile throws off heat, smoke and flame, and
draws to itself the atmosphere, which, rushing in, combines to increase the conflagration. This rushing in is
but the baptism of matter with fire, which cannot exist
without. The body may be likened to a furnace: it
must be fed with fuel; and the atmosphere must
meet that fuel in the system, or no fire is kindled
and no heat generated. The lungs are the bellows
which fan the fires of life. The pores of the body are
escape pipes. The atmosphere is the aura or spirit of the
earth, and all things on the earth live by inhaling it.
Thus it may be seen that the spirit of one thing may support another. Spirit absorbs spirit by combination, the
same as fire absorbs the atmosphere.

The body may be likened to a horse-shoe magnet, or
a combination of them. The legs are suggestive of one ;
the arms of another. We are, in fact, a combination of
magnetic motors—or, possibly, a galvanic pile. May not
our food furnish the alkali, the atmosphere the acid, the
union of which sets free the spirit (fire) of food, causing
motion, heat, combustion, growth, and life. May not
the liver correspond to the zinc, and the lungs to the
copper plates of a battery? Connected by acids and alkalis in the system, a current is evolved, which dissolves
and decomposes food as fire does wood. The fire thus
set free from food becomes the aura (spirit) of the organ-
ism in which it was set free. Thus our spirits are made

up in part from that which we eat. There can be no
combustion without the union of matter and atmosphere.
That union is the fusion or blending of all forms into one,
and that one is formless, viz., fire or spirit. Power resides in the formless. In the imponderables there is
freedom, and without freedom there is no power manifested. To a spirit in bondage there is the darkness of
matter, but a spirit set free is living light, an immortal
fire, which consumes matter as the light of a lamp consumes oil. GOD is FIRE, for " GOD is a SPIRIT, and they
who worship Him must worship in *spirit* and in truth."
Matter is but fire that is quenched. All it needs is baptizing with a spark from GOD, and it begins to burn and
glow with life as embers in a furnace glow with light.
There is not an atom in the body that is not vibrating
with the electric or magnetic fires which animate all things.
It is, indeed, burning with a lurid and weird intensity truly
amazing. And we might behold the grand and sublime
spectacle if it were not for the obtuseness of our dull and
materialistic senses. If once beheld, we would no longer
wonder at the vast amount of fuel required daily to support this ethereal flame called life.

The light emitted by these walking furnaces—these
torches, these living machines—varies in intensity and
volume, according to the nature and quality of the matter in combustion. Some lights are electric, radiating far
and near; so it is with some men. Others, again, are
small, and emit a soft, mild light. Others, again, give out
only a spark ; but most bodies are so undeveloped that the

fires of life smoulder, and emit nothing but a fitful gleam now and then, amid vast volumes of smoke.

This light emitted by all living beings—nay ! by all things mundane and supermundane—*is the spirit.* It is the spirit of matter in combustion which constitutes the aura of plants, animals and men. The laws of combustion are the laws of the universe, and they are the laws of magnetism,—action and reaction, attraction and repulsion, an outgoing and incoming current—this is all. Hang a gold coin on the positive pole of a galvanic battery in a solution, and a piece of brass or copper on the negative pole in the solution, but not in contact with the coin, and the result is, the positive galvanic current dissolves the gold and carries it over to the negative, where it is deposited upon the piece of brass. Electro-magnetic physicians know that they can *increase* the vital powers of any portion of the system by the application of the negative electrode thereto ; and that they can *reduce* the action of any part by the application of the positive.

Thus it is demonstrated that matter is dissolved and carried from one part of the system to another, where it may be deposited, or even carried out of the body. Now, we know that the female principle is the productive, or the principle wherein matter is combined into forms of life, and that the masculine is the principle from which such life or matter comes in solution, as the gold from the positive electrode. Every human being is a magnet, which evolves a positive force from itself, which dissolves and appropriates to the body material of various kinds from food, and conveys it to renew the decaying tissues, while it also repels and eliminates that which is devitalized. But the negative principle or force is not evolutive, but receptive, in which the positive deposits its burden of spirit. Thus is the body constantly renewed by a process little thought of, viz : that of impregnation and gestation. All motion is magnetic; and this is only another name given to the manifestation of fire—*combustion*. All things are in a state of combustion—some gently : this is growth and progress; others with intensity, as a conflagration, in which the body is reduced to ashes, and the life of it back " to GOD who gave it."

If attraction overbalance repulsion there is a slow combustion, a smouldering of the fire, in which other forms of matter appear (charcoal for instance). This is exactly the case with nature; the half-extinguished fires of life preserves the form for a space of time. But notice the slow and certain change of form from infancy to old age, showing that repulsion is master after all. If repulsion overbalance attraction there is a rapid conflagration, and forms of matter disappear in smoke, vapor, heat and flame, *to nothing*—"not even to the blue sky." It is to attraction that childhood owes its ruby cheeks and lips, and its exuberance of life. The immortal fires sparkle in its eye, and glow in its soft and rounded flesh through which it shines, ere SHAME has come to crimson the cheek and brow with a more lurid light, with a more intense combustion, in which the forms of youth change rapidly. To repulsion we owe the lustreless eye, palid cheek, the grey hairs and wrinkles of age; aye ! the death of the body comes through excess of repulsion. A proper balance is marriage, in which more things are generated than has yet been dreamed of.

The aura or spirit obeys the same laws. The positive contains the seminal principle, which it deposits, when it meets the negative, which immediately returns to the body (the womb) with its new found treasure, with elements of spirit that combine in the system with positive elements, forming new blood, new tissue, new vigor. Violent combustion is destructive to forms of matter, but the compounds resulting therefrom are of incalculable value to mankind. The ashes of wood are a compound resulting from combustion, but how much of its chemical properties come from the atmosphere is not known; nor is it known how much came from that invisible fire or spirit which resides in a negative state in the air we breathe and burn. Science, a great thing in the eyes of Professors, but is a mere infant as yet. It may be a promising baby, but it still needs nursing. The body is condensed aura or spirit, which liberated by motion flows around it as light flows from a candle, passing out positive and returning negative. The condition of the matter (body) in combustion determining the brilliancy and power of the light. Of the constituent elements of the body, science says there are many, and goes on to name them. But, gentlemen, with all respect for your knowledge, your analysis and tests, your acids and crucibles, I must say I question your conclusions. Why? Because a dead body is not the same as a living one. The moment it is dead it is in another *condition;* the elements are changed and continue to change till there is nothing left of them.   Analyze a dead bone, (you cannot analyze a live one), and you get compounds to which you give names; but names prove nothing.   In your crucible, retort and receiver the spirit of the universe is adding it-self to your work ; *in fact, it is doing the work itself.* You do not know how much of your own spirit enters into combination with the elements you are manipulat-ing.   Then why such a parade of knowledge ? We don't yet know the first letter of the alphabet of science.   Take a tub of earth and weigh it ; then in it plant a seed. After a time you will have a tree ; remove the tree, and again weigh the tub of earth, and see how much less it weighs. You will find that the tree is made up almost entirely from the atmosphere ; which, indeed, is the spirit of the earth.   Forms are a condensation of the invisible.

The earth is none the less for having produced inani-mate and animate things.   A mother is not made less by child-bearing.   The light of a lamp is not lessened by lighting other lamps.   The human brain is not reduced by giving thought and ideas to the world, but its capacity is increased thereby.   It is said that "man is like a candle : when the light goes out he is no more." I do not agree to this.   Light is an effect of combustion ; so is the *mani-festation* called life.   But light is greater than oil, as spirit is greater than matter, or as motives are greater than acts.

V.—THE MIND.

We have many so-called sciences of mind, prominent among which is phrenology. This is recognized as a science by most thinkers. The brain is recognized as the organ of the mind, and mind is treated of as an entity— the soul. I regard mind as an effect of organization. It is a something the soul has developed to enable it to come in contact with, and to handle matter. The idiot has no mind, but he has the power to suffer and enjoy. Now, it cannot logically be held that sense is mind, or that instinct is mind; infants have no mind, but they have the *capacity to develop mind.* Thus mind is a thing that grows and dies like a vegetable. Mind is a manifestation of the soul, composed of various powers or faculties. My mind is a machine I have made. It belongs to me, as my body or my coat belongs to me. It is my property. I may be robbed of it as I may be of my money. True! When my mind is gone I am driven back, as it were, to a condition where sense remains, but memory, reason, judgment and will are not. Mind is to me what the rudder is to a ship. By the use of it I sail my frail bark over the stormy seas of this life. Without it I am drifting like a piece of drift-wood wherever the waves toss me. As a man without property is considered nobody, so man without a mind is, *in fact,* a *cipher.*

As sense is the first manifestation of the soul, mind is the second, and the body is the third. But to observation the reverse seems to be true, inasmuch as the body seems first, mind second, and the soul——blank.

Sense surrounds the soul as the atmosphere surrounds the earth, and constitutes a sensorium upon which all things are photographed, all sounds vibrated, all thoughts and emotions reflected. It is sense which separates things, holds each atom and each body in place, and establishes the relationship governing. It is the sense of a thing which constitutes it a thing. Without sense things could not exist. Without feeling there is no contact. Without hearing, no sound ; without light, no colors, no beauty nor deformity. Sense does all things : it is GOD. The awakening of our dull senses is like unto an egg in incubation. The soul is the germ. The sense is the beautiful arrangement and adjustment of vital elements hermetically sealed up in a shell (body). Without this sealing up, this isolation or insulation, this partition between us and GOD, we could not exist. These bodies stand guard over our souls to preserve individuality. They are our preservation from the Infinite. The lightnings are chained down, bottled up, suspended in liquid form in the egg, as fire quenched by water in wood, coal, or storm-cloud. These bodies are important. Their quality varies, according to the power contained therein, as the shells of eggs vary. They subserve the end of solidifying the fire into organic life. When that is accomplished the shell becomes rotten, and the fully-developed chick works its way out, into a new life, or, rather, another stage of the same life, for there is only *one life*—the life of sense or of GOD. "Except a man be born again, he cannot see the *Kingdom* of *God.*" "The Kingdom of GOD" is only another and higher stage of life, and no man can enter it save through the gestation and birth of a DIVINE BODY. Ah! the mysteries of being. Thou insignificant egg! Thou holdest in solution the incomprehensible mystery of GOD and eternity! In thy darkened chambers GOD is waiting! Thy spherical form speaks of revolution as the primal law of all being! "Hermetically sealed"—so secure from curious eyes, so full of "the elixir of life," and yet so fragile! Thou art the flame-tip liquified! Pure, beautiful thing! Containing in thyself infinity, soul, mind, body and spirit! What doth thy hatching signify if it be not immortality? Thy wings speak of flight and liberty, thy lungs of inspiration, thine eyes of light, beauty, immortality and the beholding of it. Thy instinct speaks of intuition and all knowing! Even the hovering of the HEN over thee typifies the "brooding" care, and life-giving power of the Holy Spirit! Art thou evolved from the "black muck," thou pure, white thing? Can mud see? or can it make eyes like thine? Can it think? or can it evolve a thought 'or a thing capable of thought? *Or, rather, didst thou not descend*, little chick—as descends the glory of the night—from "the mystery of the shadow?" As an egg in incubation receives heat, first in the shell, and secondly in the albumen, so do impressions come to the mind through the body by *contact* with the outer world. The heat which causes growth of vegetation,

animals and men comes from without, and it is through
pressure, contact or impressions. Nature is to man what
the hen is to the egg. Physical contact is required to
warm up and influence things that have little sense; but
to those who have mind, there is a spiritual contact or
impact, far more potent and far-reaching. It is considered that man has five senses: feeling, hearing, seeing,
smelling and tasting. But I claim that there are many
faculties of the mind, and only one sense. Sense is
nearest the soul, the mind comes next. *Through* the
mind the sense receives the fire which quickens the germ
in the soul, or the egg. Sense may be said to be feeling.
We see a lovely flower—we feel pleasure. If it be
some horrible sight we are pained. We may see it at a
distance, but the effect is the same. We come in *contact*
with that which we see, hear and smell, as much as we do
by taste or touch. We see sights that electrify us. We
hear sounds that startle and urge us to action, as much
as if we had been struck a blow. We come in contact
with things and phenomena at a distance by sight and
hearing, of things nearer by touch and smelling, but it
is all feeling after all. The nerves of taste are only a
little more acute than those of the hands. We smell the
aroma of a rose, and we know it is near, although it may
be hidden. We are in contact with the rose, for we have
received something from it that has made an *impression*
upon us. Its spirit has met ours, and entering in, has
added some fuel to the fire burning within. New combinations have been formed within us, and the rose has
· added its fire to ours. Our spirits glow with a purer

light from the contact of love and beauty. All things grow by pressure, contact or impressions. The impressions we receive in our journey through life, from the gentle caress of love to the discord and clash of opposing conditions, are but for the reception of that Divine fire we worshipped in the past. Each object we meet imparts its fire ; each experience we have, from the joys of a mother's heart to the despair of the hopeless, is from the pressure mother nature gives, as she warms and hatches her brood. If we live properly we grow stronger and stronger in all that makes the true man, till the rotting shell (this body) bursts, and we fly away to realms of immortal life.

Pressure comes by attraction, and this produces growth by the gentle heat generated thereby ; but the contact which comes by force is from repulsion, and is death by conflagration. Fire struck out by force is destructive. By attraction we receive what we need, but by force more than we need, and often that which is sickening. Ask the pale, sickly mothers of the land if this is not GOD'S truth ! There is a mental or spiritual contact of things, whose limit is unknown. It is not possible for us to think of a thing, principle or state of being that does not exist somewhere, within or without the domain of " nature." To think of a thing intensely is to see it in the mind ; and this sight is clairvoyance. To see a thing is to feel it ; this is contact, pressure, *impressions*. The pressure upon the brain of a thinker shows the power of thought and its contact. The pleasure he feels in giving birth to that which he hopes will do the world a great good, shows the baptism with fire we read of in the Scriptures. Thought is the lightning's flash. It penetrates. It is the sunlight. It warms and gives color to life. It dwells in all things, for all things are suggestive of thought. They provoke us to think. If we will not think, they send the plague, the famine, and a slow decay. There are *some* rotten eggs in every nest. Thought calls us out from ourselves, from our knowledge of our weakness and follies—and then we are great. To dwell in thought among the stars is to be in contact with the GODS, and to receive from them what otherwise we should not have. Thought is a stimulant: it intoxicates. To be drunk with thought is to provoke mirth, like any drunken man.

The sun illumines a little space on the earth, but the darkness is before and behind, and all around. Like a coward it flees away as the sun approaches, and like a coward it follows close behind, as follows the past upon the present. We cannot stand still: we must move on. The little thought we have flashes out into the darkness before and behind. Memory looks back at the gloom of almost forgotten joys, and from the dim twilight of the past come the ghosts of evil deeds. Our weakness and follies appear gigantic. They are alive and active, but the little good we have done is scarcely perceptible—is feeble, is crowded back, like a small boy in a crowd. Thought flashes a ray of hope—of prescience; and the world follows its light with a deathless trust. For it, they tax themselves to build churches and to support an army of priests. For this ray of light, this spark of

Divine fire, they go hungry and in rags, patiently. Who shall say there is not a pressure here, a contact as close as that of matter, impressions that move the souls of mankind? We gain knowledge, laboriously, in the collection of facts; but these facts must be digested by the mind before they can be of use. Thought, reason, analysis, are the stomach of the mind. Here the fire is extracted from facts, as life is from food in the physical stomach. Doubt is indigestion. He who digests the facts and phenomena of life, and still doubts the immortality of man, has mental dyspepsia. He does not get the fire, and consequently his spiritual nature lacks warmth. He who properly digests the facts of life grows warm and tender, and stronger in his trust towards others. He dreams of immortality, for its fact is impressed on his mind. In his dreams the mind becomes telescopic, and he sees that which the doubter scoffs at. But, nevertheless, he grows stronger and stronger in his belief.

Long years ago I became very much interested in clairvoyance. I wished to attain the power. I read much and thought more. Sat in "circles," used magnets, insulated stools, galvanic bandages; in fact, exhausted all the methods within my reach, but with the exception of a few "clouds" and "flashes of light," my spiritual sight remained obscured. It was late one stormy night in winter, in the little cottage on the hill, overlooking "the father of waters," that, after having lain on a couch for an hour as usual, with a huge magnet in contact with my head, I retired to bed, feeling sad and low-spirited. I lay for a time listening to the moaning and wailing of the winds, and pondering upon the subject which at that time engrossed my entire being. All at once I became conscious of a presence in my room. It was intensely dark to the natural eye, but I saw clearly an old man, tall and majestic, with a lofty brow, deeply plowed with thought-lines; mild, gentle expression, long, white beard, and hair that fell on his shoulders. He held in his hand a brass rim, inclosing a circular glass. He held it up and asked me to examine it. I did so and found it a mirror. He called my attention to the fact that it not only reflected objects, but *retained* the images impressed thereon. "This," said he, "is the human mind, which ordinarily has the power of Reflection and Retention" (memory). He then pressed his thumbs upon the glass, holding the rim with his fingers. It sunk with much difficulty under the pressure to the depth of the rim. The glass then seemed a shade smaller, but was still enclosed as before by a brass rim. I looked in the dish-like mirror, and it seemed clouded; and strange, fanciful objects flitted across its surface. Again he applied the pressure, and with some effort the disk became deeper. Again I looked; the clouds had partially disappeared, and dimly seen, deep down in the mirror, as if in the far distance, a lurid light sent fitful gleams across the surface in the mirror. Said he: "The mind, like this mirror, has the power of *elongation.* Like this, the two first sections are very difficult to start; but these accomplished, and the rest come easily." And he shoved rim after rim out to the number of *seven*, and then bade me look. I looked, and lo! the wonders of the universe were revealed. The light was clearer than the brightest I ever saw. The ineffable glory of creative principle flashed like lightning upon my brain. I could not bear the steady flame, and turned my wondering eyes to the face of " the STRANGER." He smiled and said : " The mind has a telescopic power, little known to mortals. When once attained, there are no secrets that may not be discovered." And then he and the "Magic Mirror" were gone. But I have not forgotten the lesson.

In these pages, if you can comprehend the ideas, you will find a verification of its truth, and the guide-posts on the road to power. We can never know a thing or principle except by contact therewith. Ideas grow in the mind as vegetation grows in the earth. Thoughts are the letters of a word ; the word is part of a sentence. A complete sentence or a combination of incomplete sentences, contains an idea. The word is the beginning of speech, or the first materialization of an idea. Hence ST. JOHN says, " In the beginning was the Word." Now we may think and think till we are exhausted, but if we conceive no idea, and think it out to a clear and perfect definition, it will do us no good; it is like a plant struck by frost, or withered by drouth. But if, in our analysis of facts, we conceive an idea—no matter how vague—and dwell upon it in thought, it gradually takes form and grows to maturity. Maturity is a perfected idea. When an idea is matured in the mind it enters into the soul, and becomes an integral part of the thinker, and he is changed thereby.

We are changed by our thoughts. That which leads us upward towards the good is expansive ; hence, creative of power : but that which is debasing leads downward, and is contraction, hence destructive to power. The soul expands by fire, but contracts for want of it. Fire is power; and weakness is for want of it. It will be seen from the foregoing that the mind occupies an important position.

Everything that reaches the soul must pass through it in the form of ideas. For the soul is an idea itself, and nothing can enter the soul that is foreign to it. Fire is the spirit in which ideas reside. If man were natural, there could be no progress, for he would be in a state of indifference. But, being unnatural, he is progressive and *intense—i.e.*, insane in his mind. The real appears to him as unreal, and the unreal as the real. From this cause he looks upon the body as the man, and the mind as the effect of the body—like "the blaze of a candle" —and laughs at the idea of a soul or spirit. This state of the mind is termed natural. I call it unnatural. But we cannot help being unnatural on account of our *ignorance*. Ignorance always blunders—weakness always falls. The first act of the natural was a fall, for he was ignorant. When fallen he struggles to stand erect, for he has knowledge of an erect posture. The unnatural is progressive.

The mind is not a thing, but rather a law or mode of action of the soul. It is a duality—"two in one." The natural and rational are the TWO, which, united in harmony, are the DIVINE ONE. The Divine is first of all—the sensorium of the soul, as evidenced by the intuition and innocence of childhood, and the instinct of animals, etc.

From it comes all that exists. In the creation of man
instinct was suspended by a reversal, or depolarization of
it, in which it was dissolved as it were and scattered, and
became the seeds of many faculties. Each and every
faculty of the mind has instinct as its foundation. This
scattering or division of instinct may have been, and undoubtedly was, a slow process, occupying many ages.
Man is the only thing that comes into existence totally
helpless, totally blank of intelligence : hence it must have
culminated in *his* creation. The tossing waves of instinct,
torn from the depths of creation's ocean, tossed to mountain heights, and beaten to froth, subsided in a great calm !
Anon, a breath of the Infinite fanned the great deep, and
man sprang into being ! This calm is a great rest of nature as she gathers her forces for another effort; it is the
soul as it expands; the vacuum that provokes motion.
The tornado was coming ; all nature held its breath in
expectancy ! It came in the shape of mind. Ever
since its advent there has been no more calm. From sun
to sun, from star to star, from pole to pole, from centre
to circumference, there is agitation. Nature seems torn
from her moorings. Her steady and quiet ways seem
broken in upon as by a GOD. She is all turned topsy
turvy. And she, good dame, has joined in the mad
revelry, as at her own nuptials. Nature seems to have
departed from her usual methods ; an innovation has been
made, as if the absent Lord had returned, or a god had
descended ! From this point—from this great calm, this
rest and expansion, this BIRTH—work is the law. The
first effort was a failure because there was no guide, no

knowledge. *A failure!* Such a thing was unknown to
nature. Astonished and bewildered, the soul shrinks and
collapses in giving the awful thing birth ! A failure ! If
being forced back from multiplicity to unity—if being
compelled in a new creation to go back to the starting
point—indifferent sense—to work outward again to multiplicity—if this be a failure, then man is a failure. And
every man who weeps over the weaknesses, follies and
sufferings of poor benighted humanity, recognizes it as
such. Every man who has an idea of improving the race
knows there is something wrong. But nature, like an
over-indulgent mother, says to her child : " It is no failure, my child ; try again." And sinking herself in her
great love for him, becomes the *involuntary powers* of
her child. For her spoiled child she bears patiently
every abuse. She breathes for him while he sleeps. She
labors as he directs; while he, visionary that he is, is busy
building castles in the air. She walks, if he says walk ;
he takes no thought of the distance or the steps: all
he has to do is to direct her. If he fails to point the
way, through forgetfulness, she goes astray, for she seems
to be blind ; but she keeps on walking till he says stop.
If, in his perversity, he takes up some habit that will eventually ruin him, she adapts herself to his whim, and carries
it on without his volition, even to his death ; when he forgets it, she reminds him of it. In his sleep she still labors
for him to restore the waste of his unnatural life ; still
whispering *" Try again."* If he hates, she keeps it in
his mind. If he resolves to commit some crime, she assists him as readily as to do a good act, always whisper-

ing, " *Try again.*" If an incurable disease attacks her
child, she fights for him while he directs, and in the *manner* that he directs, but when he loses control she joins
forces with the adversary to hurry on the work of dissolution. Even in death she reminds him of his habits.
Nature seems to be a blind force, and *indifferent* thing,
if it be a thing. She knows nothing, feels nothing ; she
simply furnishes us with the power to think and feel,
whispering, " *Try again !*"

It is no fiction,—the fall of man,—but it is an allegorical representation of a truth : or, in other words, the effort
of a great mind to explain the life we live—the principles
of being. The acts we do furnish the light of experience.
The man who trusts in himself and walks out boldly gains
the most. He who trusts in GOD, although the happiest,
gains the least knowledge. If we fall and hurt ourselves,
we have the freedom to climb up again. And though we
may not climb back to the same place, we may go higher.

Ever since the " fall," man has been scaling the pre-
cipices of his weaknesses and failures. The point I call
your attention to is this : All acts have their beginning
and inception in the mind. Hence all violation of law,
with their attendant pain, disease, weakness, and death,
spring from mind. *All violation is a creation.* Hence
all creation is a MENTAL PRODUCT. As acts flow from the
mind, so matter flows from the mind ; for acts materialized are matter. This being so, the more Divine the
mind is, the greater will its creative power be. The evolution of matter from itself having any quality or form,
or the dissolving of matter already formed, by the sus-

pension of atomic laws, is logical, and within the range
of man's power, as a DIVINE BEING.   As a creator, all
creation is in his grasp, and he is therefore the architect
of himself, and his heavens or his hells. The conception
of a thing is the beginning of its growth.   Hell grows
out of our minds : so also does heaven ; but hell is largest.
So also a Divine body may be grown by conception, gestation and birth in the mind.

Hell is fed by our desires to see our enemies suffer, and
from a spirit of retaliation and revenge.

VI.—THE DIVINE MIND AND BODY.

The natural mind is the common mind. It receives its impressions through the five senses; or, in other words, wholly from external nature. To it belong observation, memory, and reflection. All things of this mundane sphere reflect themselves upon the mind as in a mirror. This mind grows and expands by the collection of facts, but the conclusions of it are material as the facts themselves. For this reason the natural mind cannot conceive of a spiritual or future state of existence; its utmost powers enable it only to reach the plane of knowledge, or the manipulation of matter. The knowledge gained by it is the sciences and philosophy of material things; it adapts man to this "bread-and-butter life." Its analysis is destructive; hence to it belongs doubt, skepticism, unbelief, and the impossible; pride, lust, hate, fear, avarice, deceit, and invention are its controlling powers. The interior of this mind being closed up, there is no reflection from any other way than from without. The soul is denied, because it cannot be seen or handled; its presence is unfelt, by reason of the hardness and opacity of the natural—or, more properly, the unnatural—mind.

It cannot feel from within, but is conatantly drawn outward by sight, sound, and contact. It is the "wide-awake" mind. Its highest faculty is the invention of machinery, building of railways, cities, etc.,—all of a material character. But it is progressive, inasmuch as it expands by its stretch after the new, and its effort to perfect that which it conceives.

Conception is always superior to the production. The true artist fails to come up to his ideal, because the colors in his mind are pure, while the colors of his picture, being a compound of matter, are dead. It is a mere material thing, void of soul. If he could, by looking at the canvass, project from his mind the picture he sees in his mind, project the colors from himself—without brush, paints, or pencils—on the canvas, it would come up to his ideal. This power does not belong to the natural nor to the rational, but to the DIVINE MIND.

The Divine mind does not exist to the natural mind, because it cannot come in *contact therewith*. The natural develops into the rational, which expands to the Divine. The natural, by expansion, opens the interiors, through which impressions come from the unknown. If these impressions are not rejected the mind becomes luminous. This illumination is rationality. Impressions from within awaken the mind as with a new life, and it gradually turns within—thus reversing itself. This is the beginning of magnetization, which is a turning inward of the eyes and the sight—the beginning of the glory.

The natural may be compared to the flint, and objects to the steel. The fire struck out is a mere spark, which

vanishes away and is lost; but the rational is a steady
flame, flowing from the Divine, making malleable and
luminous the entire man. Seeds deposited in the earth
first soften, then enlarge, before the germ can come forth.
The natural mind is the seed planted in the soil of the
body, but the rational is the tree; the fruitage is the
Divine; which, indeed, grows not out of the ground, but
descends, as the Spirit, to bless all who partake thereof.
This is the bread that comes down from Heaven, of
which if a man eat he shall not die.

To the rational belongs the innocency of childhood,
with its simplicity and credulity. Instead of sagacity
there is intuition; instead of deduction there are visions
and revelations. One might naturally think that rationality came with age; and so it would, if there was no
retrogression. Our daily lives cloud the surface of the
mind with a film, through which the flint scarce penetrates; hence there is no fire evolved by the friction
incident to this life. We become insulated during the
mad rush for wealth, and the magnetism that gives
growth and expansion passes by us. The real age and
life of a man dates from his conscious progress in the
good and pure. The real death dates from the time one
becomes conscious of being bad, and does not forsake his
evil ways. There are some children who are older in
soul-growth than some old men or women. There are
some persons who retrograde from earliest childhood;
others progress for some years, then turn downwards;
others, again, are bad in early life, then suddenly, or
slowly, turn to progress upward. We may pity the old

person who is hard. Progress softens the mind, and thus the whole man expands. The Divine mind is first; next is the rational; the last and outermost is the natural. The natural corresponds to matter, the rational to spirit, the Divine to soul. The Divine mind is the sensorium of the soul, which surrounds it as a translucent film, which expands and contracts. Attraction expands it; repulsion contracts it. It is the sensorium that is the seat of consciousness; the events of life are all photographed upon it. All the emotions that are experienced give color to it. The various strains of music and discord leave their impression on it. The voiceless universe affects it also. What we have been in previous states of existence is brought forward by the sensorium into this life; and the sound of the voice, the build of the body, the facial expression, the laugh, the color of the eyes—all these, and more, tell what we have been doing, and what we have been in the long eternities of the past.

Upon the inner surface of the sensorium ideas exist— in the " Holy of Holies," wherein GOD's voice is heard. Upon its outer surface symbols of those ideas are projected, which, descending into the rational according to its condition, as descends the ovarian egg, there becomes impregnated by the nature of things. The nature of things is the spirit of things, viz: Fire. The spirit dies in the impregnation, and is born (after gestation) into the natural mind *reversed—i. e.*, instead of being spiritual it is material. *It is a mere reflection of the Divine Mind,* a reversed image, as your face in a mirror. For this reason we get no absolute truth. Ideas are reversed and distorted from having been impregnated by *the spirit of what has been.* In the same manner SPIRIT is changed into MATTER, and becomes part and parcel of these bodies. For instance, you have a wound ; the pain is a telegram to the sensorium of the soul ; the idea to restore, though unconscious to you, is immediately projected by the soul into the sensorium, or Divine mind, where it meets spirit and is impregnated, and, descending, deposits life in the form of new matter in the wound. Thus are the injured tissues fed, like a child in embryo, till the parts are restored. But there is a *decay of the injured parts before and during the restoration.* How tenderly and carefully we nurse and dress an ulcer, thus causing it to give way to new and healthy flesh. Matter is but spirit reversed. Substance is substantial ; it does not change, but spirit and matter do change in becoming reversed. The decayed matter of an ulcer is the return to spirit, and matter in formation is spirit condensing : which is effected by that third and incomprehensible thing—the soul. These material bodies are but an ulcer, so to speak, upon a Divine and substantial body, which the soul is striving to free therefrom. But in most of us this Divine part is destroyed, swallowed up, eaten through and through as by ulceration. The substance of the Divine Body is *an idea of it.* Matter, without an idea, falls or lies dormant ; but with an idea it rises up and walks erect as man. Aye ! and with an idea of it he rises up to be a GOD.

Ideas revolve in cycles of time as worlds revolve in space. Hence, "there is nothing new under the sun."

We get a glimpse of the Divine in childhood and in first love: But the fog soon—alas! too soon—rises and obscures the sun. In the reversal of ideas the external, or the last, appears to be first. Causation appears on the surface of things, and life and mind seem as the effect of matter.

Religious ideas are of the soul; its symbols—being projections thereof—are *reversed* images which the world worships. The esoteric is lost in the rubbish of the exoteric, as the soul is lost in matter. But it flows on in cycles, vast in extent, and gradually works out of the rubbish, and asserts itself as miracle. The age of miracle is near at hand! The cycle of the soul is nearly completed! Already we can see the first dim twilight of the rising sun!

From the worship of the Divine—THE ONE, the first mathematical number—we have gone down to the number nine in the absurdity of addition, and now in that constellation we worship MANY GODS—our FOREFATHERS. But the absurd NINE will pass away, and the next cycle will be the union of the Immortal 1—symbol of creation and the beginning—with 0 (10) symbol of the soul. The Father and the Mother at last united, the Son (the Divine mind) will appear on this earth. Thus we revolve in a numerical circle from *one* back to one again.

The idea of heredity carries us back to our forefathers, and we lay the blame of our follies upon them; but they went back to Adam; Adam laid the blame on the devil; the devil lays the blame on GOD, who created and educated him for that purpose. Thus in thought man makes

GOD out a demon, inferior to the lowest of humanity in sympathy, and superior to the devil in cold malignity. What absurdity !

Why not accept what we *know* as the truth? We know that *our acts* make and unmake us, and that we suffer and enjoy through our own acts. What I am my acts in this life and other stages of existence have made me. I am but an action, and every act I do adds to or diminishes my power to create, to enjoy, to suffer, and TO BE. I AM the numeral ONE—the first and the last. When, in the progress of life the soul expands to the outermost being, and becomes the OVER-SOUL instead of the inner, then shall the Father (Spirit) be one with the Mother (soul), and the Divine mind (the SON or SUN, symbol of Divine light and knowledge,) shall illumine the night of matter, and all secrets which lurk in darkness shall stand out in their naked deformity. "Then shall no one say to his neighbor, know ye the Lord, for all shall know Him from the least to the greatest." This is the Trinity, and the real significance of the FATHER, SON, and HOLY GHOST. SPIRIT, the FATHER, GOD ; Soul, the MOTHER, HOLY GHOST ; MIND, *the only begotten Son* of *Spirit*, or of God. The union of spirit and soul is typified by marriage ; creation is typified by children, as the son or mind begotten. As an idea reversed or dwarfed becomes monstrous, this idea of the Trinity, Divine as a symbol, has been rendered unnatural by the loss of its Divine intent, and doubly damned by the enforcement of unnatural statute laws.

The natural becomes the rational by development, and the same is true of the rational. Many there be who do not believe in the Divine. To me Divinity is the noblest and best part of humanity—a beacon light, far above us, luring us upward and onward to real manhood and GODHOOD. All rationality is negative, but naturalness is positive.

The spirit flows out and in. As it flows out it dissolves and carries away effete or dead matter into the atmosphere, when it becomes the life of something else; this is a positive current. As it flows in it brings with it the spirit* of other things, with which it has mingled in its revolutions around the body; for, like everything in motion, it revolves. In this mingling the spirit becomes negative, and returns to the body; so all spirit that builds up the waste of the body is negative. The negative is feminine, and all formation takes place therein. Rationality is the negative mind. All art and mechanism is

LIGHT AND THE SOUL.—The Berlin Gegenwart, of Nov. 15, 1879, contains a rep rt of experiments made by Dunstmaier to te t the accuracy of Jager's theory, that the soul of every man and animal is to be sought for in the characteristic od or exhaled in each case. Dunstmaier, who unites in his own pers n the physiologist and metaphysician, was, until these experiments convinced him of his error, an outspoken opponent of Jager's views. He is now, however, an enthusiastic convert. Dunstmaier's method was no doubt suggested to him by his familiarity with experimental science. He considered that light and the soul—if the soul is an o lor—a e both radiated, and that light can be, as it were, collected and fixed by a photographic plate covered with iodide of silver. What body, now, is as sensitive to odors as iodide of silver is to lig t? Evidently the nerves of smell in a dog. In the centre of the laboratory a cage containing twenty hares was placed, and a dog was admitted to the room. He at once made violent efforts to get at the hares, which, of course, in their terror, rushed to and fro in the cage. After two hours of this torture the dog was killed, the nerves of smell and the mucous membrane of the nose removed, and rubbed up in a mortar with due to rationality. All aggressive acts and destruction is due to the positive or natural mind (as I have termed it in this chapter for the sake of simplicity). The Divine mind is that incomprehensible and out-of-the-way mind —that *third thing*, standing guard between the two, wherein they meet and become one. Now, this meeting of the spirit with matter, and its transformation from spirit into matter, is a strange and mysterious thing. The spirit itself is not life, but it contains the germ which comes to life in the *third* thing, which contains in itself the power of generation. Mind is the connecting link between matter and spirit—hence it is in the mind that transformation is effected. This mind becomes Divine by unfoldment, which, indeed, is nothing more than a union of the natural with the rational. In the way we look at things from without, the Divine is evolved, but in reality the Divine contains the natural in itself, and is first in the order of creation. There is Divinity in all

---

glycerine and water. The twenty hares had been exhaling their souls for two hours, and the dog, during all his panting and sniffing, inhaling them for the same length of time. The glycerine might be expected, then, to contain a certain quantity of the soul of the hare, the main characteristic of which is, of course, timidity. That this was the fact the following experiments seem to prove: A few drops of the extract were administered to a cat; she ran away from some mice instead of pouncing upon them. By the subcutaneous injection of only two cubic centimetres a large mastiff was rendered so cowardly that he slunk away from the cat. By a similiar experiment, in which, however, a young lion in a menagerie played the part of the hares, Dunstmaier succeeded in isolating the soul substance of courage and in transmitting it to the other animals. Still more interesting experiments showed clearly that these "psychotypic" glycerine extracts had a decided effect on the human species. Thus, after swallowing a small dose of psychotypic timidity, Dunstmaier had not the courage to believe in his own discovery. This effect soon passed off, however.—*London Medical Record.*

things, as there is life in all. We speak of the mind as a thing, having an organ, the brain, and a location therein, but we know of no such thing. The mind may, and probably does, come to a focus in the brain as a great centre of perception; but I have good grounds to maintain that it occupies every atom of the body—even to the toe-nails and hair; and that it surrounds the soul, separating the spirit from it, and that it is the great laboratory of the Infinite, in which spirit is transformed, and matter receives its quickening power, and is transfigured, transposed, or rendered up to the Infinite as an incorruptible substance. JESUS was in possession of the Divine mind. It was not possible for Him to be sick, to suffer pain, or to die, save as He willed it. He did not die, only in appearance; neither did His body ascend, only in appearance, but was transposed. This transposition is a vanishing away out of sight. Read of the transposition of Philip, in *Acts* viii., 39–40. Andrew Potts, of Harrisburg, Pa., told me—and the same was corroborated by several truthful men who witnessed it—that he vanished out of the sight of his friends at the depot, when they were about to take the cars for a town six miles down the road, and that when the cars arrived at that station he was already there, talking with a friend who was waiting for the train to escort the friends to his house.

JESUS' life and death was to show mankind that He was the same as they, and to show them the possibilities of human nature. A teacher, to be acceptable, must not be too far removed from his pupils. Had JESUS manifested the powers of a GOD, vanished from the cross, etc.,

He would have converted the Jewish nation in a day, and they would have worshipped Him as God. But what good would that have done? Lo! the world has been worshipping Gods for countless ages, and some portion has been worshipping Jesus ever since His crucifixion, but what good has it done?

The Doctrines of JESUS are sublime in their truth and simplicity—but very much, of the most value, has never been penned. It has been urged against him that he taught that which, if practiced, would subvert *civilization*. On the contrary, it would redeem mankind from barbarism and idolatry, and make men civilized in place of semi-savage. "Greater works than these shall ye do, because I go to the Father." "By their fruits shall ye know them." "These signs *shall follow those that believe*." Who believes?

It is the weakness of matter which compels it to lie dormant and still in one place ; this it is which causes it to fall down when not supported. Gravitation is only another name for weakness. So it is with mind. That which is under law is weak, and the more materialistic the mind is the weaker it is, and the more bound by law. Mind is law, but the thing moved and governed is matter. To fulfil the law, then, is to *perfect* the mind, and the matter under it; for law makes matter, and imparts every quality to it—motion, weight, buoyancy, etc. To the perfected mind all mundane things are under, or enclosed in it, as a large circle encloses smaller ones. There is no such thing as perfecting nature—it is already perfect. Neither can an imperfect thing generate a perfect thing. The imperfect changes by rising up to, and receiving the perfect within itself. Thus the wise man works through nature, not against it ; and mastering its modes, methods, laws and minds, transcends them all ; and looking back, becomes a spectator rather than an actor. This is the fulfilment of law, or in other words, the being *filled full* of mind. For as we ascend in the scale of power, we become more and more *involved*, or enveloped in mind,

which, penetrating through and through, illuminates the
spirit, and gives buoyancy and fluidity, or malleability,
to the matter composing the body; thus connecting it
with other matter, to influence, control, mould and fash-
ion it for use, as one uses his hands. In order to pass
from one nature, or mode of existence, into another, generation and birth are necessary. *This involves a sleep.*
The spirit worlds are of *this* nature. In order to go beyond them—to the realm of absolute power, the germs of
the mind must be ripe. We are here for the purpose—
some of us, at least—of generating mind ; not merely to
spend a few years in amassing wealth, or in toiling to
support bodies. Those in whom the mind is not half
generated remain in this nature to try it over and over
again. Unripe germs will not grow. To pass into the
nature or " Kingdom of *God,*" a *regeneration* is necessary, because it is an incomprehensible nature to this finite
mind—hence the entire man must be re-made. The
body is of no account. Mind is that which *determines.*
Some minds are of no account. Fate determines. The
truly generated mind may, and does, regenerate the man,
and endow him or her with supernatural power and immortal life, here on this earth. That which ensues at the
death of the body is simply generation, and not a regeneration ; for in the regeneration the body is changed in
quality consciously, by the joining to it of the Divine
Mind. There is no sleep or trance in this; it is effort;
not physical, but mental effort, in the destruction of
things that disturb the harmony.

There are many enemies to human progress, prominent among which are the following of a downward or retrogressive series, which are antagonized by an upward or progressive series. They may properly be termed Powers—one of Light, the other of Darkness.

Powers of Light.	*Powers of Darkness.*
1. Revelation.	1. Ignorance.
2. Joy.	2. Sorrow.
3. Temperance.	3. Intemperance.
4. Continence.	4. Concupiscence.
5. Justice.	5. Injustice.
6. Communion.	6. Covetousness.
7. Truth.	7. Deceit.
8. Good.	8. Envy.
9. Light.	9. Fraud.
10. Life.	10. Wrath.

—Hermes.

Revelation may be known by its imparting a great satisfaction, rest, or joy to man. Joy is prolific, since it is the feminine of ideas. As Revelation drives away ignorance, so joy drives away sorrow—or prepares the mind to resist sorrow, and to be self-sustaining in its completeness—to stand calm and tranquil amid life's changing scenes, and be content and happy despite adversity. Temperance in all things is revealed as the source of health, and immediately is siezed upon by the mind, and when it has grown apace, *Continence,* the feminine of it, is evolved. And they two drive away *Intemperance* and *Concupiscence.* When this is accomplished the mind is as clear as a polished mirror. The turbid waters of selfishness and lust have subsided, and *Justice,* stripped of vindictiveness, stands revealed as mercy, and becomes the ruling power of the mind. Then comes *Communion*, the feminine of *Justice*, and *Injustice* and *Covetousness* flee away. There is now no feeling of "mine and thine" left in the mind. All things are pure, and all things are common. The communion of the sexes, of races, of *spirits*, *angels*, and *Gods*, is effected, and the mind trembles with its fulness upon the confines of absolute truth or oneness of being. The soul has now ascended to the seventh sphere, and is pregnant with male and female twins—"the *Truth of Good*, and the *Good of Truth*," which in due time are born into the conscious mind, whereupon deceit and envy take their departure. In the light of truth all distinctions and differences disappear, and all things are good. But this light reveals another light—dimly seen at first—far away upon the backgrounds of the soul—fitful and fleeting, obscured by passing shadows, it grows brighter and comes nearer—an *immortal light*, in the centre of which is the germ of another life—of an immortal substance called "the Tree of Life." It slowly enters into the mind, and descending from thence enters into and transforms the changeable matter into a substance at once homogeneous and not particled. The man is no longer in light and in life, but light and life are *in him*. The Infinite is no longer without and far away, but it is within; not divided and separated from, but the integral part of all being, tangible, visible and intelligible. The impossible does not belong to this life, and flees away upon its approach, or is not. The darkness and ignorance which forms the background of the soul, in which we are hidden from ourselves, has been withdrawn, and we are revealed as the *Over-soul* itself, containing all life and forms within. We are no longer involved in law or mind, for we contain all of these, and are conscious thereof. And we use them as we now do our hands and feet. Man is master of all his soul embraces. This is the proper generation of mind, wherein the body and spirit are regenerated. To such, death is not, for death is a weakness. The intuitions of a ripened mind are as broad and deep as the universe, but those of a small or an unripe mind are weak and shallow. Hence the necessity of mutual culture—not in the acquisition of earthly knowledge, but in the effort to grasp creative power—philosophy, astronomy, etc., in their broadest and deepest aspects. Philosophy is the highest of all studies. It wings the soul. Truth is so little known that it is folly to waste words in argument; but speculate, think, entertain and master all ideas thereto; imagine, grasp at the Infinite Mind, and bring it into yourself, for in the effort the mind expands, stretches out and grows. What if you accept an error to-day? You can change your opinion to-morrow! Above all things, beware of fossilization.

Had Jesus healed the whole world in a day, it would have been sick again in a few weeks, if not days. He did not teach worship, but *manhood*, as a Divine thing. He taught salvation as flowing from *works*, and not from *his* merits or blood, or from the worship of him, or anything else but principle. He taught the influence and value of belief; and also of several kinds of baptism—of water, of fire, and of the Holy Ghost; and also of a baptism which he should undergo at his death. We are left to conjecture what baptism he meant when he said, " He that believeth and is baptized shall be saved," etc. (See Mark, xvi., 16, 17, 18). But we are not left in doubt in regard to its being the baptism with water, for the Christian world has been "sprinkled," "poured" and "plunged" in water for eighteen hundred and eighty-two years; and *where are the "signs"* he said should follow as an evidence of salvation? He said he was the bread of life; to eat thereof was to be immortal. Now, the truth is, he was teaching the same thing I am trying to illustrate, and his ignorant apostles, or some one else, have got it mixed up and distorted, in order to deify *him*. He said the bread of life came from heaven; and also that " the Kingdom of God is within you." He also spoke of another birth, and of *sight*, as a result of that birth. Baptism with water is a symbol of purification in order to the reception of another Baptism, viz., that of fire. The Baptism with water is typical of the softening and the making tender (as a seed) the natural mind, so that it may expand or revolve in its growth towards rationality. The softened, tender, sympathetic, open-ing mind, inhales the fragrance of another life, and it buds, blossoms and bears fruits which are a blessing to all. Its blossoms are a sight of the kingdom of *God*, and its fruit is the entering *into* the spirit of all truth, and the birth of a Divine Body, indestructible and eternal. Bathing assists the will in the healing of the body, and in the subduing of the heat of passion. Water opens the pores of the body—belief opens the mind; the first for the reception of magnetism (spirit), the latter for the reception of ideas, which are, indeed, of the soul (H̲OLY GHOST).

This is the building up of a divine body of a supernatural substance, from the atmosphere of a thought-world. We need not die, if we only know how to live. But what can we say of a world of men who think of nothing but vanity, and for the serious part of life hire the thinking of it done? The thoughts doled out from millions of pulpit-grinders every seventh-day are but the effluvia of the past, the exhalations of the dead. What kind of substance do they furnish for a dying world? Is this the "bread of life?" Is there a spark of original fire in it? He who depends upon books for his *inspiration* is but an exhumer of the dead. The heavens are as open to-day as when Isaiah, gazing aloft, said, "Lo, I am God! and *I change not;* therefore, ye sons of Jacob, are ye not devoured." The same power is waiting for us to reach up and take that existed in the olden time for him they nailed upon the cross. The tables of the Infinite are spread, and loaded, but no one will be compelled to partake. Help yourselves, is the universal law.

At the tomb of Lazarus, in view of a body lying stark and dead, with the smell of death, and the mould of the grave on his pallid lips, with eyes that gazed the Infinite out of countenance with their unflinching audacity, *He* of the magic *Will* said, "If a man believe in me he shall not die." Did he mean physical death? Most assuredly he did. Take this as corroborative: in speaking to the Jews at another time he said, "Your fathers did eat manna in the wilderness, *and are dead;* but I am the bread of life which came down from heaven, of which, if a man eat, he shall not die,"—meaning the same death the fathers died in the wilderness, viz : physical death. And yet, in the face of these positive declarations of the *In-spired One*, the pulpit organs grind out a spiritual explanation. They make JESUS' work apply to a future state, when he intended it wholly for this life. The Hermetic Philosophers, the Alchemists, and the Rosicrucians, have all believed in and taught the doctrine of eternal youth, and sought for the "philsopher's stone," and the "elixir of life ;" and JESUS taught that life was within the Kingdom of heaven, which "is within you;" and laid the foundation-stone, BELIEF.

The fakirs of India cause a shrub to grow out of the ground, blossom, bear its fruit, and ripen it, all in one short hour. And it is no phantom fruit, for it is passed around and divided among the bystanders, who eat thereof. Scores of travelers have witnessed this feat, and many have written of it, but my authority is a gentleman of veracity who was born and reared in India. It is done under circumstances which utterly preclude the idea of jugglery or trick of any kind. They know and say it is the power of the will that does it. But there is no growth to their power. Why? Because they have no higher ideas of human powers than the manipulation and production of things. They are not a progressive people. They are at their highest point. It remains for the Anglo-Saxon race to go higher ; for it is a higher race.

JESUS said, "Greater works than these shall ye do, because I go to the Father." And it would have proved true had they made the conditions. It remains for us to make the conditions, which are, to work for that baptism with the *Holy Ghost* and with *fire*, viz: the union of spirit and soul. Water makes the body soft, tender and pure. Baptism is to be submerged, swallowed up in the spirit, which is the beginning of a new life with wondrous powers, generative of new matter—a divine essence, superior to death and dissolution, which in appearance resembles this body, but which, in fact, is not mortal. It was this body which JESUS, MOSES, ELIJAH, PHILIP, ENOCH, and several ROSICRUCIANS of the olden time are reputed to have had. This was why JESUS said, "I will lay my life down; *you* CANNOT *take it."* This Divine body may die, if *corrupted by the desire to die.* Thus ST. JOHN could live, notwithstanding he was plunged into a cauldron of boiling oil, till he *desired* to die. The Divine body is not a spiritual body, hence it is no apparition, or materialized form dependent upon a medium and conditions. It is totally subject to the will, and as it is projected *from* the mind, it may be drawn back into the mind again, and thus disappear. Or it may change and become *some other form.* This was why the Disciples failed to recognize JESUS on the way to Emmaus. "He appeared to them in another form," says MARK. But when he had blessed the bread and broke it, he was himself again, they recognized him, and then he disappeared. At another time he stood in their midst, and as they doubted, he said, "Feel my flesh and bones, for ye know a spirit hath not flesh and bones." The doctrine of the metempsychosis of the soul is as true as it is old. All things are in the divine mind, and are projections thereof by Divine WILL and Love. Hence, man, when he rises to the Divine, has the same powers, so far as he is concerned, as an individual. Thus, he may clothe the naked, feed the hungry, heal the sick, raise the dead, walk upon the water, still the tempest, or visit the GOD-worlds at will. When that good time comes we will not need to take thought for to-morrow. Then we can " give to every one that asks," and "he that would borrow" we need not "turn away." Then " whatsoever ye shall ask shall be granted," not because ye ask in anybody's name, but because then we may say with JESUS, " I and my Father are one." Then there shall be no high and no low, but as brothers we shall dwell together, and the nations shall learn war no more. Then shall " the lamb and the lion lie down together," and " the knowledge of the Lord cover the earth as the waters cover the great deep." Then good-bye to mammon and to a civilization whose glory is " an eye for an eye and a tooth for a tooth,"—" whoso sheddeth man's blood, by man shall his blood be shed."

VIII.—ATTRIBUTES OF MIND.

That which can be ascribed to the mind is an attribute thereof. We have to do now only with a few. In my view, all things mundane may be attributed to mind, but distinctions are necessary to illustration. All attributes of the mind are dual—"Male and female created he them." They antagonize each other; one leads upward, the other downward—or inward and outward. All development is in expansive curves, from one to many; then in contractive curves, back to one again, of a higher or lower order. Nothing moves in direct lines. The expansion of the soul is her effort to *gather* power; her contraction is her effort to *use* that power. This is focalization. All power, to be of use, must be focalized. Intellect is the *eye* of the soul, which must be focalized in order to attain clear sight. The rays of the sun in *diffusion* gently warms, and brings out many hidden forms from the earth; but in *concentration*, fire is evolved, which consumes or obliterates these same forms of matter which were evolved by its gentle rays. Even the granite mountain would vanish away as a vapor, if the light of the sun was all turned upon it. Yea, more! even the solid, beautiful earth would evaporate into the imperceptible—not even into blue sky—if the sun's forces were all turned upon it. Focalization is the destruction of the old, and the birth of the new. Intellect corresponds to the sun,

not only in form, but in power. It is to mind what the
sun is to the earth. Its darkness is ignorance, its light is
the birth and life of many things. The diffusion of its
light causes the mind to radiate into many channels, or
attributes, in the growth of which the soul is expanded.
But intellect is not satisfied with this ; and when it isdis-
satisfied it begins to contract itself for another and a
mightier effort ; it turns all its light upon one point of
the darkness, which, like an opaque night, surrounds and
pierces through—as a burning of it into another life, or
another method of this one. This is the begetting of another intellect (intuition) from this old one, which has
been consumed, or left behind as a charred and blackened
ruin. The door of intuition once opened, there is no more
use for observation, memory, thought or reason ; its light
penetrates the depths of all mystery ; language becomes
automatic ; and, without thought or effort, ideas flow in as
the waters of a mighty river ; all reasonable needs are
supplied as if by magic. To such, if any there be, I can
say, with JESUS, '' Take no thought of what ye shall say,
neither take heed for to-morrow.''

Man, considered as a whole, is the focus of all forces
beneath and above him. The essential qualities of all ani-
mation are in him, and find their focal point in the mind ;
hence the mind is composed of instincts, *disunited* or at
war with each other, the harmonious union of which is
the beginning of a new order or genus. *Intuition is instinct humanized.* We scarcely know what intuition is.
There is plenty of sagacity and instinct in the world, but
very little intuition. To it belongs all the spiritual gifts

we know of. Intuition is the seed of the tree of life. All seeds attract heat, moisture, etc., before they can project the shrub or tree; hence, the first law of intuition is attraction, which is the feminine, or the law of all mediumship. All inspiration, prophecy, healing, clairvoyance, clairaudience, psychometry, and all other spiritual manifestations, come by attraction. I am aware it is a physical condition; but the body is affected by our mental states as a thermometer is affected by heat and cold. Attraction depends upon *attention*. As a mother nurses her child by constant attention, so an attraction depends upon attention. As a tender mother nurses and cares for her only child by unwearied watchfulness and attention, so are the gifts of the Spirit obtained and perfected. Intuition is the seed of the tree of life, and the various attributes of the mind which lead to gifts of the Spirit are its trunk and branches.

The loftiest mind has not yet fathomed the depth and height, and multiplicity of spiritual gifts. They are all attributes of the mind, which, ascending spirally in cycles from the natural to the rational, at last bask in the bosom of the Divine mind. It is all within, waiting the baptism of fire, which comes by action. " Dead here, slumbering there, latent in all save a few," we look upon it as miraculous; as a manifestation especially ordered by Deity for a favored few. Mediums arrive at a certain stage of development, and there stop; then wonder why the gifts gradually die. (See chapter on Mediumship). The mind is a trinity in unity; that is, it is animal, mental and moral. The external mind corresponds to physical nature, and is called the animal ; the intellect corresponds to fire—the spirit ; the moral corresponds to the soul. There are seven attributes of the mind, each imparting a certain quality peculiar to itself. They have their antagonists, as follows :

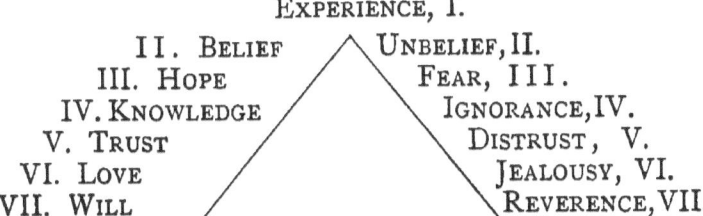

EXPERIENCE, I.

II. BELIEF	UNBELIEF, II.
III. HOPE	FEAR, III.
IV. KNOWLEDGE	IGNORANCE, IV.
V. TRUST	DISTRUST, V.
VI. LOVE	JEALOUSY, VI.
VII. WILL	REVERENCE, VII.

To the mind belongs quantity and quality. Quantity gives momentum, but quality gives elasticity and buoyancy. The attributes of the mind each has its antagonist, as shown in the above diagram. They both grow out of experience, but they are as opposite as day and night in the influence they exert upon us. Each exists by opposing the influence of its opposite ; the life of one is the disease and death of the other. There is not life enough in the mind to feed them both to fulness, so they strive with each other for the lion's share.

The fundamental principle of this life is experience. To it belong observation, memory, thought and investigation. We all begin and end with experience ; if we try, we cannot escape it ; we *must* experience something. The experiences of some, however, are as trivial as that of a root which grows in the ground ; according to the experience, so is the growth. We revolve in circles in our growth. Every experience is a circle—a triangular circle, of which belief, hope and knowledge are the angles. Knowledge is the ultimate of every act, of every experience, and is twofold in its effects, viz: good or bad. It either adds to, or diminishes, human happiness. The nature of the knowledge gives it its effect, *i e.*, it imparts a certain quality to the mind conducive to happiness or misery. That which imparts rest, peace and tranquility is conducive to health and happiness ; but that which causes dissatisfaction, unrest and agitation, conduces to disease and unhappiness.

BELIEF AND HOPE.

The great fundamental principle of Christianity is " Believe, or you will be damned." This presupposes that man has power to believe as he *likes*. This is undoubtedly a truth, as regards *some* men, while there are others who are controlled entirely by evidence, or, at least, by what appears as evidence to them. To convince a man of a truth, it must appear to him as a psychological power. It must appear so fascinating as to carry his will captive through his love ; then the evidence supporting it will appear very plain and logical. When the antagonist of belief overbalances belief, *i.e.*, when persons are of a skeptical, doubtful, incredulous turn of mind, they are, as a general thing, not easily influenced ; they are inflexible, and become fixed in opinions to which they become *devoted*. This devotion is the same out of the church as in. It closes the mind upon all sides, save the one through which they look. They become bigoted in their one idea, which is a creed they are bound to sustain. Unbelief is the beginning of strife. It is a contradiction, and strife is sickening. The unnatural man fights for his opinions and against the opinions of others; but the natural man loves repose, and is indifferent to opinions of others. Strife is of hell, and perhaps it is good for the unnatural, but there is no health or life therein. Now, unbelief, being a negation or contradiction, it has within itself the spirit of agitation, which sets in motion discordant mental elements, antagonizing belief, which is of the soul—of intuition—the condition of childhood. The spirit of belief is that of childish innocence and credulity—of trust, hope and confidence. Hence it is peaceful and restful to the soul—so expansive. He who does not believe in immortality fails to do so because he feels not the pulsating heart of GOD within himself. Let him who believes keep silent till he knows the truth and can demonstrate it, if he desires good results to himself. I do not believe in strife, but let those who do, join battle.

That a man cannot believe except from evidence, is true; but one man receives evidence from without, while another *feels it within*. *We cannot accept a thing as truth except it be in harmony with our inmost feelings*. He who really believes in GOD believes in his own power to become God-like; but he who believes in the devil *knows* of him, for he *feels him within*. We all instinctively believe in that which we love. We believe in that which harmonizes with us. Mental assent is no belief;

it may be forced out by fear, or love of appearance, or popularity, or gain, but the real belief is what we live. In view of this, Paul says, "As a man thinketh, so is he." Belief is the fundamental principle of soul-growth. The credulous man stands higher spiritually than the incredulous. Why? Because all growth and real power depends upon the absorption of Divine fire, and belief opens the pores. All magnetizers are aware that belief and fear cause receptiveness. Fear is based upon belief. The belief in the "harmful Gods" has diseased mankind through the cold, malarial influence of fear. We do not fear that which we know; it is the unknown we dread. True belief also gives hope, and hope casts out fear and imparts cheerfulness. Belief in that which we fear is not a belief, but an apprehension that the thing threatened, though unknown, *may* be true. This apprehension or fear creates a trembling and quaking as of an ague. It is disease.

He who believes in himself reposes in himself, and achieves success; but he who doubts himself is afraid of his shadow, and achieves nothing. Achievement is the acquirement of knowledge—as riches. But he who achieves nothing, knows nothing, and is poor; hence he is dissatisfied with himself and others. He who knows least of himself trusts himself the least, and is afraid and doubtful. As of himself, so of others. We judge others by ourselves. He who has the most trust and confidence in others has the best and highest knowledge—first of himself, secondly of others. He who knows the most of money knows the least of mankind. He trusts money, but not manhood, for his knowledge leads him to distrust mankind. Knowledge gives confidence or destroys it. Woe be to him whose knowledge diminishes his trust. Remove the little confidence we have in each other, and all friendship and sociability would cease. Nations and governments could not exist, and progress would be at an end. Confidence is the diviner part of us. It is the child-nature—that which is " of the kingdom of heaven." Woe to him who has little or no confidence in mankind, for he has none in GOD. Sleep is sweet to the trustful soul, for GOD dwells within, and bars the door of darkness through which devils creep when we are off our guard. I have heard men boast of their doubts, of their unbelief and incredulity. But to me it is an evidence of smallness of mind. Religion has become the laugh and grimace of the world, by reason of the want of comprehension of its votaries, and of the unbelievers. He who worships symbols is an idolater, and rightly provokes the mirth of others; but there is something sublime in *principles* which always commands respect. The underlying principle of all religion is the same, and is as old as humanity. True, out of this principle—this fire-faith of the olden time—has grown up dwarfed and hideous forms of religion, at war one with the other, as man wars with man, or nation against nation. But the principle is still Divine, and universally breathes of the brotherhood of man, and the FATHERHOOD of GOD. Who is there who, in contemplating the wonders of creation, has not felt the leaping of flame thoughts, as if in rapture—the kindling of a divine fire within that leaped and glowed with a fervent heat, melting our hardness of nature, our skepticism and unbelief in the wisdom of creative genius? Ah! who has not gone hence from this closet of worship feeling like a coward, humbled and weak as the publican and sinner who smote upon his breast, and cried, "Father, forgive me, a sinner!" I repeat, it is the small-minded, weak man, who quenches the fires of his own soul by his doubt and skepticism. To gaze aloft at the stars and rear not out of your own soul a spiritual temple of principles for the guidance of life's actions—for the use of mankind—and instead, only spend our time in tearing down the house wherein our neighbor worships, is unworthy of manhood. Power is that which builds anew—not that which destroys. It takes genius to build an edifice, but a rat might undermine and topple it to the ground. Doubt, skepticism and unbelief are so many walls surrounding us, isolating and insulating us from each other, and keeping us far from the realms of power. In proportion as we know a person to be truthful do we trust; their love for truth is natural; and it is our nature to believe in truth; and whenever we find it, we trust it, and hope for its increase and perpetuity; and when we know of it we love it, and will its spirit to be ours. Belief, hope, knowledge, trust, love and will, are all of kin to truth, and hé who cultivates these graces shall yet be filled with righteousness. Hope is based in belief. "It is an anchor to the soul." In proportion as I believe a thing do I hope for its truth. In proportion as I believe in others do I hope for their health and prosperity. We rest in our hopes. The grave looks less desolate to the hopeful soul. Cheerfulness and smiles are hope's children. The unbelieving are the hopeless and the dissatisfied, he who believes in nothing, hopes nothing ; the hopeless are the desperate. Which road will you follow, dear reader, for the truest knowledge? Do doubts and skepticism stand in your way, and choke and strangle belief? Destroy them, then, by not paying attention to their croaking. *Forget* your doubt by keeping in your mind and constantly before your eyes that which you love, or that which you would like to believe in and be. It is by the attention we bestow upon little things in the mind that makes impassable mountains of them ; forget, or refuse to behold them, and they become *mole hills*.

Have you an enemy—one whom you can scarce endure ? You know no good of him. This feeling does not make you happy—better destroy it speedily. Visit him in his prosperity and in his affliction *frequently* ; talk with him ; interchange ideas with him ; enter into his life-plans and hopes. In process of time you will find some weakness in him that will arouse your pity, which is not far from friendship. The ingredients necessary for success in this is, first, a *desire* on your part to bring about the result, if for nothing else than your own peace of soul ; second, a *belief* in your ability to accomplish what you undertake ; third, a *cheerful hope* of success ; fourth, a true *knowledge* of *yourself*—of your self-control, and psychological power, and of extraneous means to affect him physically, such as gifts, or good and unobtrusive acts.   My word for it, before you are done with your man you will be surprised at the amount of good feeling and friendship that will be developed between you.   Perhaps he fancies you have done him a wrong.   If you can possibly find some flaw in yourself, go and accuse yourself to him and beg his pardon ; accuse *yourself* for the very things you know *he* is guilty of, but never accuse or upbraid him.   But if you do this with doubt and unbelief in your heart of any good in him, your eyes will look your distrust, and he will be driven away from you as from a reptile.   Control begins at home.   Which road will you follow, reader—belief or unbelief, in order to make the most of yourself?   Which leads to power?

KNOWLEDGE.

It is said that "knowledge is power." This may be so in one sense, but let us examine and see wherein it is true. There are different kinds of knowledge, some of which are a destructive power. The knowledge of this world is based on facts gathered through experience. All the facts known have reference to matter, and things related thereto. So the relationship of things is the sum total of human knowledge as founded on facts. Is destruction power? It is not reasonable to call that power which destroys health and happiness; in fact, weakness is a more fitting name for it. Of course, there is force manifested in destruction; but it cannot be said to come from knowledge. To illustrate: In the construction of an edifice, some mistake, blunder, or oversight, leaves a defect in some important part, and after a time, in some manner—even in the settling of the building it falls to the ground, and in a moment the labor of years, notwithstanding the knowledge of many skilled artisans, may be ruined through the weakness of ignorance. Shall we say, then, that ignorance is power? It would be just as logical as to say that *knowledge* is *power*, *unless* it can be shown that knowledge has some real and lasting benefit to confer. Is such the fact? Is there anything real in our much-boasted knowledge? Man's happiness and health is of more importance to him than anything else in existence; and that which will confer the greatest amount of these upon the greatest number must be real power. It is claimed by the church that the knowledge of GOD will do this. This, indeed, might be the case if there was any such knowledge in existence. We know nothing whatever of GOD! Nature we see every day, but all any one actually knows of *it* could be put in a very small compass. All we know is that which happens under *our immediate observation*. That which happens in one place may be known to a few persons in that locality; but that which happens in another place is unknown to them. So, it is easily seen that that which any one person actually knows of nature and its phenomena is very small. The most of what we *think* we know is mere hearsay. In the sciences even, we shall find the same weakness. Chemistry is based upon experiments made during past centuries to the present date, which experiments, indeed, illustrate wonderful mysteries. But what is really known save the effects of certain combinations? A person learns how to produce the phenomena, and to repeat the names, etc., of the chemicals and the products, and he forthwith imagines he possesses a wonderful amount of knowledge, and is immediately dubbed "Professor." The bulk of the knowledge is in a long catalogue of *names* intended to mystify the ignorant to the glory of the "Professors." It is certainly a great thing. For gunpowder was invented; forthwith war became a "science." "Military tactics" are a great thing ! The possession of this knowledge helps a man up wonderfully ! To be "major," or "general," or "colonel," is to be up in the clouds ! They tread upon the earth as if they disdained it; butchers, pillagers, ravishers ! the destroyers of peaceful homes ! What a power ! The science of government is built upon the blood ye have shed. What a store of knowledge it takes to be a legislator, governor, president or king ! To make laws to hang the lowly, and to enable those who have knowledge to escape. Look you at the vast sums of money spent yearly to keep the government of even one State running. (Now, we are not regretting the money, but are thinking of the aching limbs and backs that toil year in and year out to support this cursed display of knowledge.) For why does this government system exist? So that millions of soldiers may be kept in worse than idleness ; so that hosts of the so-called great may live without toil; so that the ill-gotten gains of the rich may be guarded, and they *protected* in their legalized swindling and high-handed robbing—so that the millions may be kept subservient to the few. All legislation and governments are based upon the false and illogical *assumption* that "the dear people" need *force* to compel them to do right. Is not this assumption based in *ignorance* of the real character of mankind ? What kind of knowledge is it that springs out of falsehood ? It is a lie from foundation up. Look how you have multiplied legislation till the *law books exceed* the *brains* of the *world*. Law is now a *science*, about which its professors differ as much as the professors of theology do

about religion. To keep this hydra-headed monster alive
colleges are built and sustained, wherein the most
promising youth of the land are immured to bleach, fade,
and grow prematurely old, in order to earn--what?
Legal quibbles, technicalities, and precedents, whereby,
in the great majority of cases, *justice may be defeated.*
In the great (?) courts of law the best talent is generally
arrayed *against* justice, and in favor of wrong. Law
signifies rule, and rule signifies a king and "nobility"—
false distinctions among men. Why do they exist? So
that the few can fatten upon the toil of others ; so that a
few can ride in coaches, dressed in the finest fabrics,
while the many can walk, (or "tramp," as it is now
fashionable to call it), and go in rags. A short time ago,
I saw a man lying under a bridge. I asked a Methodist
"divine," with whom I was talking, why that man was
lying there? "Oh! I don't know," said he; "I suppose it is some tramp laid down there to rest. I have *no
use* for *that kind* of people." And the law is for the up-
holding of that spirit. They nailed the poor "tramp"
of Galilee upon the cross in the olden time. Ah, me !
What a world of knowledge this is. Chemistry has given
birth to the science of medicine ; another assumption
based in ignorance. It assumes that disease is a thing of
the body, and that physical substances—drugs—have
power to cure it. Bah ! The more medicine you take
the sooner you die. The whole system is mere guess-
work. Anatomy and physiology may be termed sciences ;
but they are merely the observation of the body. When
it comes to the application of their facts to practical

utility, aside from surgery, "humbug" expresses its real knowledge. And yet, see how the arm of the law is thrown around its army of cormorants and extortionists to *protect* them in their robbery of the ignorant toilers. You tell them that all diseases spring from the mind, and that the vital forces and drugs can never cure, and they stick up their aristocratic noses with a sneer and a laugh. What a wonderful science! Then, again, there is the CHURCH; what a power it is! "By their fruits shall ye know them." What are its fruits? Its basic principle is the authority of a musty old book—"the BIBLE"— over which a ceaseless strife is kept up as to its real mean-ing. Thoughts, and legends, hearsay narratives, so-called facts of the long ago, called "holy." An assumption of an overruling Providence who answers long-drawn words, accompanied with "holy" hands uplifted, and eyes turned upward, in public and in private, to be seen and heard of men; a Providence who loves some and hates others: an idea at once at variance with the sun that shines, and the rain that falls, and with every instinct of a true human being, and which all nature, animate and inanimate, stamps as an assumption of ignorance, based in the lust of RULE. A pretence of holiness, and of humility, to conceal the rottenness of greed, lust and pride. Its principle is that of king-craft and priest-craft: the few ruling, and living by the toil of the many. Church, science and State—a trinity of HELL in which DEVILS are hatched. Pride is the floor of it. Is it igno-rance or knowledge? Knowledge gives the power to rule; but it is the ignorance of the masses, and of the many honest and good men who preach and uphold this thing, which is the foundation. There may be some knowledge about it; but ignorance exceeds it, as the sky exceeds the small earth. This assumption of HOLINESS is a falsehood from first to last, and its direct influence is to create the feeling that one man is better than another. " Am I not a child of God? And you are a child of the devil. Lo! I am better than you; because I am holier than you, and GOD loves me, and hates you." Such is the *unspoken voice* of the christian world; *but it sounds very loud.* One day is to be kept holy; but the other six are unholy; the days of toil—of the production of the necessaries of life—these are unholy days; idleness is holy! What a mockery of true manhood, and the truth! No wonder the world runs mad with the idea to get rid of toil! The church teaches that it was a curse put upon man. Of course, he is at liberty to escape it if he can, and the priests and aristocrats of the world are doing it upon the hard-earned bread of the ignorant dupes. Why should I feel holier at one time than at another? And how am I to enter into holiness? To be happy is to be holy, and mankind find their health and happiness in the alternation of rest and exercise. Is one any holier than the other? " All nature says *no,* and he who teaches differently simply shows his ignorance. JESUS was of the same opinion. When we speak of knowledge, we speak of truth. JESUS was dumb when asked, " What is truth?" All knowledge is relative; there is no absolute knowledge. So knowledge, in order to conform to truth, must deal in the relationship that man sustains to others.

Now, inasmuch as there is only an approximation to knowledge, man must depend upon his *perception* of the truth as his guide to the *basis* of such *relationship*. This perception comes through much thought, and is an intuition or a revelation of the truth. So, power, to be of *use, must* be *guided* by *perception* or *revelation*. This comes to man by the exercise of his mind—in freedom. Revelation to one man will not do for another, except as it helps him to see ; nor will the revelation of one age do for another ; for the race progresses, or grows beyond the perceptions of a previous race. Now power exists ; but it is no more in knowledge than in other attributes of the mind of equal radius. Kindness may have but little knowledge of itself, and yet we all know there is more moral power in it than in mere knowing. Knowledge is of no use to the soul save in the opening of the mind to a perception of the true relationship of things. In the lower orders the law is for the strong to prey upon the weak ; but man, in proportion as he rises above the brute plane, comes under the law of EQUALITY, and it is revealed to him as a great truth. His knowledge of his relationship to others has changed, and he now no longer preys upon the ignorance and weakness of others. The LAW is EQUAL RIGHTS in FREEDOM. He knows now that power comes through union of feeling and brotherly love, which no knowledge on earth can give. Knowledge is not power, but it is the road to power, if you can find it ; but that which seems to be the road may be a blind. The experiences of life all have a tendency, when looked at rightly, to wean us from its toy shows and vanities.

Facts are of value only in this. The swift-fleeting years rudely tear the illusions and delusions of youth from every true man of mature age. What, in reality, is the knowledge of this earth worth beside the bed of death, or at the grave? The half-witted clown with an abiding hope and confidence in spirit-life hath more power under such circumstances than all the millionaires in the world without. Power is in self-sustaining calmness—not in money, nor in knowledge. The knowledge that binds a man to this life by the development of pride, egotism, and self-sufficiency, is a curse, and a source of weakness instead of power. The knowledge that makes one all alive to the woes and misfortunes of others lifts him out of the soulless laws of business, and upward to a recognition of the fatherhood of GOD and the brotherhood of man. This is the knowledge that gives power. This is the knowledge that sustains in all trying hours.

Such claim very little knowledge, but much love. The knowledge of this world—of matter and its laws—are for this world, and are true to our senses while in it, but are not applicable to other worlds or other senses. It may be—nay, it is possible—to develop senses in this life adapted to another mode of existence, where pleasures are real, and life is earnest and enduring, and your sciences of no account, and your gold as vapor. Is such knowledge real power? Yes! but it is not knowledge, but a gift of the Spirit through the death of these sublunary things. It is not of the intellect, but of intuition.

Oh, how blind and dumb we are! We behold the miracle of the rising sun daily, or feel it in a perpetual

motion within and around us ; but instead of being de-
lighted at having discovered the finger-marks of the Infinite, we say, "Oh, that is natural !" Child-like, we are
satisfied with a name ; that ends the discussion ; "I *know*
what that is ! That is nature."

Men of science will explain the laws of digestion with
a flourish of names, and wonderful erudition ; but what
does all this knowledge amount to ? Diseases outgrow
your remedies. We do not know why food in one
stomach changes into elements to sustain life, and in
another is converted into acids and filth. Indigestion !
Ah ! another name to explain away ignorance, and to
shove GOD further away from recognition.

Such is knowledge—an excuse to hide our shame—our
ignorance. We do not know how much or how little the
Infinite adds himself to us, or withholds himself from us in
our eating, drinking, sleeping, waking, thinking or talking. But when I tell you that the vital substance of these
bodies comes from the intangible—the unknown and immaterial, the supernatural—instead of from the food we
eat, you say, " That is all theory ; that is speculation or
conjecture." I grant that sientific knowledge is good
enough so far as it goes—and that is merely to combining
and compounding matter for use—and the use has proved
destructive to man's best interests. It has filled the world
with egotism, materialism and unbelief. It teaches that
death is a *fact*, *fixed* and *certain*. But it will yet be demonstrated that death is a mere disappearance, and that the
disappearance is not a fact except to the blind—blinded
by this world's light. Knowledge is the basis for conjec-

ture. He who does not believe in conjecture is an unbeliever, (trusts only in facts, physical, tangible, and shuts
the windows of the soul through which we may gaze upon
fields of infinite beauty, and behold truth in its purity), and
there rests *satisfied.* He who believes nothing except
what he knows, is a very small pattern of a man, for in
point of reality he *knows nothing.* The man who
ties himself to "facts" is like a fly in a spider's web:
he is not satisfied. There is a wail within him,
as of a drowning babe. It is only when he can forget
himself and his doubts that he is happy. When you have
gone through the whole gamut of experiences, and find
reality and permanence in nothing, and vanity and vexation of spirit as the sum total of this life, you have then
reached the plane of knowledge. This takes the egotism
out of a man. He is then empty and receptive of Divine
influences, and is led to *trust,* and to have *confidence* in
creative wisdom. Trust leads to love of GOD IN HIS WORKS—
not of objects, but of a principle embodied, and working
in objects. Thus it may be seen that the road to power
starts at belief in GOD. He who believes has Hope.
Hope is cheerfulness and happiness. Truly we believe
in that which harmonizes with our feelings. To believe
in a thing through fear is not belief in this sense, but
rather a conviction of experience, far beneath belief. It
is a shock, an agitation, wherein there is no rest or satisfaction. All conversions through fear testify to this truth.
He who is converted through fear has no intuition; hence
he is not called from above, but from below. Intuition
does not come from without, hence no practicing can

awaken or open it. Instinctively we fear that which is not in harmony with us. How, then, can we believe in that which we fear? We always desire to destroy that which gives us pain. The fear of GOD is a pain which the world tries in vain to remove by sacrifices, prayers, and flattering ceremonies. Fear does not lead to knowledge, or blending of natures, but to unreal and erroneous views of GOD and of each other. It builds walls around us, as a citadel in which to defend ourselves. It isolates man from his fellows, and arms nation against nation. We fear that which we hate, and love and serve that which we are in fellowship with. Fear springs from belief, but it is in a descending scale: it is beneath and not above. The fearful are not the hopeful. Hope is the anchor of the soul. It is GOD's garden in the soul; the Eden wherein the tree of life and of knowledge grow side by side. With hope, the poor in their hovels can live in palaces built in air. Without hope, the rich in their palaces live in *real hovels*. Conjecture is stirred in the mind by the last expiring wave of heat that descends from Divine fire, as it deposits its ashes as the facts and forms of existence. Belief is the flame-tip; hope the glow of the red flame; knowledge is where the flame bursts forth; unbelief is cold ashes. Right belief is belief in man, and it inspires hope in man, and gives a correct knowledge of man. This is a correct knowledge of GOD. How can we believe in GOD when we do not believe in man? How can we have hope in man when we fear him, and hold aloof from each other? How can we know GOD when we really do not know any *thing* in existence?

I. Let us investigate all things; for this is experience.

II. Let us believe in all things; for there is a spark of good in all, and the wisdom of the Creator may be found therein.

III. Let us hope all things; for the good manifests itself in hope. Be of good cheer, for all is well. The hopeless are desperate.

IV. Let us know all things; for the essence of things is fire; and he who knows the most is the purest, having been purified of his pride and vanity by the absorption of the essence of things.

This is the mundane circle — the four elements — the four points of the compass. He who has passed around this circle has returned to the point from whence he started, viz: nature—indifference. He is a child again, without pride or egotism, hence is receptive to the Divine influences, which leads him in a supernatural manner upward to the abode of the GODS. Those who return to this point are capable of going higher.

We all revolve in the mundane circle in quest of knowledge. Some gain a little, others a great deal. To some it imparts trust or confidence in man (or GOD); others grow misanthropical, and become soured on the road, and trust no one. Acid is cold; it kills the warmth of the blood, and gradually, but surely, extinguishes the fires of life. Distrust is acid. We become fixed in our opinions on the circle, and branch off, either upon the upward or the downward road. Some, however, revolve in the circle of knowledge all their lives, and still have no opinions of anything outside of the mundane circle.

It is said that only fools have confidence in mankind ;
but this is a mistake. The best and greatest men the
world has ever known have been child-like in their trust
ful nature. The rogue and the knave are never trustful.
We have existed previous to this life; and we come
here from above or below, bringing the aroma of
the world we came from with us. There are three
grades of mind, corresponding to the three general conditions of Spirit-life. This world and this life are a battle-
field between the celestial and the terrine worlds, an in-
termediate state where souls are given a chance to ascend
higher if they choose. There are many grades of being,
both ascending and descending ; and man mentally and
physically corresponds thereto. The spirit of the world
you will inhabit after death *is within you*, and as sure
as fate will gravitate to its home when freed by death.
The spirit of the terrine world begets all manner of vices
and diseases, whose culmination, unless healed, is total
loss of all power and consciousness. All love and humane
affections come from the celestial. All things die in love,
and all things are born of love. The extremity of grief is
beginning of joy. The last throb of pain is the first throb
of pleasure. Ecstacy is close upon the confines of despair. The extreme woes of hell vomit out souls purified
by fire. Extreme knowledge strips a man naked of his
egotistical garments, and shrouds him at the gate as if for
burial.

This is the death of knowledge : the state of the mind is
changed; it has reversed its polarity. His intuitions begin
to work in his despair of life, and he receives that which is

to the soul what knowledge is to the mind, or food to the body. Intuition begins where worldly knowledge ceases. Its methods are inductive, instead of deductive. To the intuitive, knowledge comes by impact rather than by contact. All revelation comes through intuition. The foregoing is the secret of all conversions. The despair of the sinner, when at its culmination, dies. Its death is the birth of ecstacy, which many mistake for the regeneration.

But it is perfectly natural that pleasure should follow pain : hence there is nothing supernatural in conversions. The deeper and more heartfelt the despair, the greater the pleasure that follows it, and the more real and lasting is the conversion. But GOD's Spirit comes through intuitions—spontaneously, by labor and constant and unwearied attention—by purification of the mind, and a preparation of the body for its reception. It is natural to believe in the supernatural, but unnatural not to believe in it.

X.—FAITH AND KNOWLEDGE.

The most FATAL enemy of the soul is DOUBT. He who doubts his own powers cripples himself. He who FORGETS his doubt rises superior to himself. He who believes in, and has confidence in himself, has more power than he who doubts his own powers. Moreover, the more confidence a man has in others the greater is his friendship, and the more friends he has. Friendship is the measure of influence, and, consequently, of power. (In order to simplify, I will only speak of belief, knowledge and faith in this chapter.) Out of belief comes knowledge; and out of knowledge comes faith, or, rather, that which approximates faith and makes it possible, viz: Intuition. *Perfect faith* comes from *perfect knowledge;* but inasmuch as we are imperfect beings, and, consequently, have no *perfect knowledge*—not even of ourselves, and still less of others—how can we even *approximate* a *definition* of faith? much less a knowledge of the powers it may confer upon its possessor! Why scoff at the sayings of Jesus, when we do not even know what he meant by faith? He certainly estimated its value very highly, for he said: "If ye have faith like a *grain of mustard seed*, ye shall say to the mountains, be ye moved and cast into the sea, and it shall be done." It is evident he coupled it with the will, for it could be done by a *command*, and no prayer or supplication is even hinted at. What great thinker ever extolled DOUBT? or taught that it ever conferred any great blessing upon its possessor? Not one! It is simply a destructive power— a negation; it builds nothing; it destroys all that it touches.

A desire to know the truth is commendable. Respect for others leads to the interchange of ideas and investigation. This is good. Never doubt a proposition till you are sure you *thoroughly understand it*. Never doubt the truth of another till his falsehood is a demonstrated fact. *Know* a thing before you reject it. Be hospitable to the wayfarer: for although you may be imposed upon many times, you may some time entertain an angel. Some thoughts are angel-sent. Said a Materialist to me: "Am I to entertain a proposition simply because you assert it? Suppose you say the moon is made of green cheese—am I to accept it? That is too absurd!" Such puerile arguments are used by pretended thinkers. It is as logical to say the moon is "made of green cheese" as that a a flower is made of mud. Either one is absurd; but the self-same elements enter into and compose the sun, moon, stars, earth, light, thought, and "*green cheese.*" Such are the arguments the doubter is driven to to sustain a semblance of logic.

Knowledge is the ultimate of mental action, and if at its highest point, or apex, it meets the spirit world with sufficient intensity to become impregnated with a *desire* for something grander, and a more lofty idea of human nature and its possibilities, with not merely an idea " to know good and evil," but to know the GOOD, and to have power to do it under all circumstances. Then, indeed, it may truly be said to be the *road* to *power*. As such I recognize it. Analyze, sift, digest all the facts and phenomena of this existence ; weigh the stars and suns of space, and trace them in their eternal voyage ; dissect the human form, and search the convolutions of the brain, and, if at the end, you have no belief in the divinity of creative power, no belief in the spirit that has escaped your telescope, your scalpel, and your scales, tell me not that your knowledge is the road to power. For real power is repose, rest, trust, confidence, and harmony. That which brings no satisfaction and rest is destructive. So, knowledge may build up the soul and expand it, or it may contract and weaken it. If knowledge makes a man egotistical and proud, it does him harm ; but that knowledge which causes one to realize how small and insignificant he is, and how very little he knows, and of how little value that knowledge really is to him, makes one negative, and receptive to the world of intelligences which surround him. Then it is that they come near and speak to his soul, and he conceives an idea of "BRAHM," "ALLAH," "JEHOVAH," "JOVE," or "GOD."

The knowledge of facts is good, for it expands the mind ; and when the mind is sufficiently expanded, it leads to deep thought, reverie, abstraction ; and abstraction opens the door of the soul, viz : the IMAGINATION. The imaginative are the credulous. Power does not come from one thing alone, but from the all—the Infinite.

Knowledge is necessary to weakness and infancy; but for the GODS there is no knowledge—it is simply faith. Faith includes all things of an inferior nature, as the ever-arching dome of heaven encircles all within it. It is beyond all knowledge; then who can explain it, or who can understand it? It is to the soul what knowledge is to the mind. As we can only approximate knowledge mentally, so we can only approximate faith intuitively. According to our knowledge, so is our faith. In exact proportion as we know wife, children and friends, do we have faith in them. Knowledge is not predicated upon anything *but truth*. It is not satisfactory to merely know that a thing is false. We must *know the truth* in order to be satisfied, and to be made whole and clean. As you know yourself, you have faith in yourself. As you *know* GOD you have faith in him. All that the mind can grasp of anything is that which appears, and this appearance is a *revelation* of something hidden. It may come in dreams or in visions, or in reverie, or in contemplation, reading of books, or conversation; or listening to sermons or lectures may provoke the conditions necessary to induce revelations; but in whatever way it may be induced, it is subjective; it is a union with the thing thought of— a oneness of spirit and being. You have faith in yourself because you are *at one* with yourself. You have faith in your wife in exact proportion as you are one with her. Faith in things changeable, and hence untrue, is destructive; because they desert you and leave you empty. Faith is a power which comes to man as a revelation, in the expansion of the soul, when the mind is closed up;

laid away, as it were, or suspended—held in abeyance.
Then things sublunary disappear, and the ineffable glory
appears; and, entering in, is one with SOUL-giving power
undreamed of by mortal man. Faith *steadies, sustains*
and *fortifies* the will; combines all spirit in one. The
powers of dissolution and of creation are of faith. It is
effortless. It is the suspension of all mundane laws.
Knowledge is of no account, only as it assists one to
enter into the Spirit. Then it is set aside, as a man
having scaled a wall, and not being obliged to return,
throws the ladder down. Think you this faith and
power can come to us? Nay! *We must ascend to it*
through a *regeneration* in the *Spirit*, and by a *birth* of the
Spirit. It is another mode of existence, to be entered
only through birth. Salvation is from weakness, disease
and death, and thus from hell; for hell is an outgrowth of
these. We work the best we can to prepare the way; but
we make mistakes and failures in our ignorance, and fall
continually. But faith is a gift of the Spirit in answer to
our *intentions* and *aspirations*. In faith there are no
mistakes nor failures. It is not possible to lose faith when
once attained. How is it possible for a child, after it is
born, to become as it was prior to birth? Faith is
universal. There is no *one* or *particular* faith. *There
is no such thing as* "THE FAITH;" consequently faith
cannot be lost, any more than GOD can be. Talk about
"falling from grace," and "losing the faith!" Nonsense! They never have any to lose. There is a fall,
however, in the pretense of possession. The pretender
always falls.

It is the habit to speak of faith as a something akin to belief—as blind—as less than knowledge. But this shows our ignorance. Faith is to the Divine mind what knowledge is to the natural. Through and by knowledge things of use are produced and multiplied in the earth. Through and by faith matter is evolved from the spirit, which, from a chaotic, formless state, takes form such as the will may determine. By this method Jesus made bread and fish for the hungry multitude. A few loaves and fishes were sufficient to furnish a nucleus of attraction, when, in obedience to his will, his Spirit flowed in and assumed the form desired. In view of this principle of evolution, he said, "If ye have faith like a grain of mustard seed ye may say to this mountain, be ye moved," etc., "and it shall be done." "First seek the kingdom of GOD, and then all other things shall be added unto you." The kingdom "is within you;" it "is at hand;" it "is like unto a pearl of great price;" or "like a little leaven which a woman hid in *three measures of meal*." The meal is a type of the body, mind and spirit. The wisdom of things is seen in their mechanism; the order and harmonious arrangement and adjustment of parts, and the ease and perfection of motion without jar or friction. The same is true of the mental and spiritual man as of the physical. The jar and friction of this life is what wears out the machine called man. Each and every atom of the body is in motion, and they are in health well poised and lubricated. This is harmony. But when there is not a proper balance of all the essentials, there is a discordant friction of parts, and a loss of power, motion, health, and vigor. The soul furnishes the lubricator, viz: magnetism. I call your attention to the fact that the great balance-wheel—the regulator, LOVE—is sadly out of line.

The kingdom of heaven is harmony, power, eternal youth, life, innocence, and peace. The principal element of the kingdom is wisdom born of love and will. If love be lacking, or be of a low, vulgar order, the wisdom born of her will be inharmonious, and the kingdom is that of disease. By wisdom, through faith, are all things made. But if the wisdom be inharmony, and the faith be small, or none at all, what can you expect to flow from the spirit; or, what *quality of life will be generated?*

Bear constantly in mind, kind reader, that when I speak of GOD, I speak of your power of will and love. When I speak of wisdom, I have reference to the harmony of yourself. Harmony means a great deal. HARMONY means ONENESS; no conflict; no opposing elements; no warfare between the flesh and the Spirit. "The lamb and lion have lain down together." Remember, health is altogether due to what little harmony we have. The greater the harmony, the more wisdom. The greater the wisdom, the more life, peace, rest, pleasure. Discord wears us out. The best of us scarce last half a century, and that length of time is enough to disgust most people of life. We are scarcely able to generate magnetism enough to keep this human machine in order more than fifty years at the utmost. Now, were the love pure and innocent, and the will strong and God-like, the

wisdom or harmony of the machine would be more perfect, and the life evolved, or the spirit set in motion,
possessed of such power that mountains might be dissolved; or bread, fish, flowers, clothing, or human forms
evoked at pleasure, and the machine possessing such
power could wear on eternally without friction or age.
"Greater works than these shall ye do, because I go to
the Father" (Spirit.) The dark and noisesome earth—the
fiery constellations of heaven, with their countless hosts,
all exist by the will of God, and are sustained by his love
and wisdom. But HE lies slumbering as in a tomb in
the things he has made. The mighty mountains piercing
the clouds, crowned eternally with purity, as a flame-tip,
tell us in their vomitings of fire—in their groaning, and
shaking, of the nature of him who sleepeth beneath.
Tombstones are they, flame-shaped and spiral, marking
the resting place of the infinite. They show the oozing
out of HIS power, and the aroma of HIS presence fills
space, things and men with his returning consciousness,
which, when fully returned, will swallow up all things as
matter in fire. The changing forms—the mutability of
things—is due to the fire which dissolves, changes, and
combines matter. The will baptizes the fire as with
water, and thus in wisdom preserves forms, and per-
petuates life. It holds it in check, and regulates the
heat so that we are not consumed. This is the esoteric
meaning of the baptism with water. If the will can re-
strain the fire through its exercise, it also can unchain the
lightnings and vomit out flame, which, though unseen,
shall not be unfelt, and which, meeting things on the way,

passes through, dissolves, and causes them to disappear noiselessly, in decency and in order. The same hidden and unseen power drove back the lightnings in their mad revel on "dark Galilee" at the simple words, "Peace! be still."

It is the unnaturalness of man that keeps the Infinite under. We cannot return to nature, but we can rise up to the supernatural, and still exist. We suffer pain, because of the deficiency of fire. How easy for the strong will to turn a flame upon the dark door of it, and exorcise it as if by magic. We are full of darkness and sorrow, because we are vacant. How easy to be full if we are only wise!

To attract the fire and hold it by baptism is fulness; which, indeed, is life-pleasure; nay! ECSTACY, beside which trance is as a dream. In purity all power resides. Fire renders all things pure. It reduces, refines, purifies, and illuminates all things. Fire flows from love. But you do not know what love is. You think it hath something of sex in it; and so it has, for sex is a symbol of it. The ecstacy of a virgin soul when first baptized by the contact of a spirit, all in harmony, is a poor expression of love in its abstruse sense. But it is the best I have. Love is not the soul; but it is the highest and most *ecstatic* EMOTION the soul can feel. It moves the whole sensorium of the soul, and by its motions evolves a spiritual fire that burns in the nerves like a volcano. As a volcano vomits out molten earth and mineral, so fire, trained by the will (baptism) decomposes all dross and baseness, which it eliminates from the system, leaving nothing but the pure metal. Beware of the fire, it you are impure ! it will leave not a vestige of you, soul, mind or body. Love builds up or destroys. Slow, lingering decay is as certain as rapid combustion. Nothing comes out of GOD's crucible but immortal beings.

XI.—THE SOUL.

" *The soul that sinneth, it shall die.*"—BIBLE.

I have already defined the soul as a vacuum, and herein appears the impossibility of it. The sublime and the ridiculous are so closely united that sometimes one is taken for the other. Modern philosophy, backed by science, says there are no vacuums; that " nature abhors vacuums"—thus virtually admitting their existence; for how can nature abhor that which has no existence? It is not possible to conceive of a thing which has no foundation or existence. The supernatural is denied, also, and that shows the weakness and nakedness of philosophy. The soul is supernatural, and it is a vacuum; but it is not given to ordinary minds to comprehend this. How can the natural mind believe in that which nature abhors? We instinctively try to destroy that which we abhor, and the mind that rejects a proposition is at variance therewith, and its thought is that of destruction.

No man can conceive of the supernatural, except he have a something in himself in harmony with the idea. The soul is a vacuum—it is supernatural, because nature cannot destroy it; and that which is hidden is always superior to that which is visible. Soul corresponds to the feminine principle in nature, but this correspondence does not make a natural thing of it at all. It is not a thing, but that which gives birth to things. Attraction is the feminine of nature, but this is not the soul, but that which the soul produces as a governing law in nature. In nature, things are moved by CONTACT and by IMPACT. Operations by contact are always downward. We cannot operate upwards, save as we receive that which is superior from above by impact. This is the way of the spirit. Spirit is NATURAL, UNNATURAL, TERRINE, and CELESTIAL, and may become supernatural by working itself out of the laws governing those four grades of spirit; or, in other words, by becoming master of all of nature's methods, operations, modes of action, etc. This is within the range of man's powers. This nature in which we exist is not infinite. There are other natures. This is a peculiar one, in which *motion* is the law. Perfection of motion is the ultimate of this nature. Perfection is stagnation, of which we know little. The perfect union of soul and spirit is the supernatural, but the spirit is swallowed up by soul in such union.

This union was called "NIRWANA" by GOTTAMA, which HARDY, the translator of BUDHISM, says means annihilation. But he mistakes. It is an existence outside and above all human comprehension. Hence the difficulty of explaining it. All spirit is fire; but spirit outside of soul has quality, quantity, sound, and colors; which are lost in the fusion or oneness of soul and spirit. "Things of the spirit are nonsense to the common mind." Soul is not a thing, save it be united to spirit, neither can we conceive of it save in imagination.

To conceive of the soul is to make a thing of it—thus man creates his own soul as a thing. Without such conception the soul is formless, and there is no permanence or reality to its existence, *i. e.*, it takes any shape, according to circumstances and conditions. To give form to the soul, then, is man's highest work. The souls of vegetation and animals have no fixed or durable form. The same is true of some men. All perfect forms are spherical, and the Rosicrucian symbol of a winged globe is a type of a perfected soul. Some Rosicrucians claim that the soul is located, or has its equator at the pit of the stomach in the solar and semi-lunar pexus, with one pole in the brain and the other in the sexual organs. This is undoubtedly true of a perfected soul. But in its imperfect state it is in every atom of the body, and cannot be withdrawn therefrom save by death. The lungs are the physical representation of the soul's wings. All flights of thought depend upon inspiration—a breathing in, as it were, of another atmosphere, from a thought-world. The perfect soul can leave the body at will, and fly away to realms more vital than this. But the imperfect is held fast to the atoms in which it is anchored by demerit. The perfect soul and spirit can make and dwell in any kind of a body it chooses, and dissolve it at will. There is a vivifying and vitalizing, exhilarating and exalting influence comes by deep and protracted breathing; but in thought there is a deeper, broader, higher, and more profound exaltation, because it touches the sensorium of the soul itself. Breathing is physical; thought is mental; but meditation is the poising of the soul's wings for flight.

There are some thoughts which take hold on the filth of hell, which they stir up to the degradation and damnation of the thinker; there are other thoughts which elevate the soul and exalt the thinker. In neither case does the thinker go outside of himself in his thought, albeit he imagines that he does. In order to become an epitome of all, man must pass *through all*, which can be done mentally; for the true man *lives in his mind*. He must dissect himself, and analyze all his passions, motions, emotions, motives, etc., and master them all. They are the steps in his ladder of progress. He must begin at the bottom to climb. The sexual and love·nature are at the foundation of existence. GOD has so ordered it that man's greatest happiness, as well as his greatest woes, spring from this source. If there is anything impure about it, it is in the mind of him who so estimates it. Of all acts the sexual is the most potent, for herein man approaches the nearest to the portals of Divine creative energy. Here, in the veiled temple of women's body, GOD baptizes matter with his Spirit, and lo! it becomes an immortal being, having in embryo all the powers of GOD himself. Is there anything degrading about this? The true man and woman love their children. The great solace and pride of their lives are offspring; they are a result of this relation, of which we may only speak in whispers, and over which a pall must be spread. As if GOD has made something of which man is ashamed. In this relation soul meets soul in an ecstatic blending of Spirits, and a watchful GOD bending low from on high "broods over the Holy of Holies" in the temple, and accepts the sacrifice, consumed with fires of love, and entering in, is born of woman. " The Immaculate Conception" is the result of a perfect union of man and woman. The resulting child must, of necessity, be superior to the parents, for such is " the CHRIST, the SON or the *living* GOD," *not of a dead one*, for DEAD GODS produce half men and women—devils in human form. " We are dead in trespasses and sins." A virgin typifies purity of Soul. " The HOLY GHOST" is " the Holy Spirit," or a pure Spirit. Now, the union of such produces " the ONLY BEGOTTEN SON OF GOD ; for GOD cannot be incarnated in impurity, save as a progressive being. The only way GOD can be begotten of man, or in man, is through purity. But what is purity? What is sin? Disobedience of law is said to be sin. Without law there could be no sin, for there would be no standard, or regulator of action. This is an idea as true as nature, and as old as humanity. The writer of GENESIS expressed it in an allegorical manner, or as a fable or parable. Law is, after all, only a mode of action. But of what action is sin predicated? SEXUAL ACTION! Nothing more, and nothing less. Strange idea ! And wherein is its truth? A virgin is pure ; but a mother—a fully developed woman—one whose love-nature has had full expression, *is impure !* I am not one to scoff at an idea hoary with age, which has had the respect and reverence of the good and great for untold centuries. This vague legend or tradition, of the fall of man, *must* have a foundation in truth, for it belongs to all races and nations. And this is also proven by the present condition of mankind, which

I have set forth under the head of THE UNNATURAL. It is a matter of little or no consequence *how* it happened, but it is of vital importance to know *wherein* the fall consists. The ancients wrote allegorically. The fundamental truths were not for the multitude, hence they were hidden away in parables, or conveyed in language intended to mislead. All knowledge of value was fast locked in the temples, and taught only as mysteries to the initiated. But in their writings the truth is manifested occasionally, especially to him who has "the keys." The ancient wise men, seers, and prophets, were deeper versed in the mysteries of nature than we are, hence some of them stood nearer to God, and received truth more in its purity and simplicity.

The fall of man was the fall of the soul from its perfect spherical form to a diffused or atomic state. To a perfect soul the emotions are perfectly subject to the will, and any part of the system may be affected in any manner desired *without the provocation of contact with objects.* Before the fall woman was a subjective or spiritual being, (taken from Adam while in a trance, as I will more fully explain hereafter)—a materialized spirit, with which Adam copulated, thus preventing her return to a subjective condition. When the soul fell to an atomic state, subjective things became objective, and contact of things became necessary to produce emotions of pleasure and pain. Adam did not need the contact of copulation to produce ecstacy, for it could be produced without—by will, and that without waste of virility. And the command was that he should not copulate. Such, evidently, were the

views of the ancient philosophers, as I will try to explain
further on. The scientific world is mad with evolution-
ism. DARWIN has sunk modern thought low down in the
mud! Protoplasm is GOD! It appears to sense that
out of mud come flowers and fruits. This appearance,
however, is the same as that the sun rises and sets—the
earth flat, etc. It is a delusion. That which appears is not
the whole truth; the most vital truths do not appear to
observation. A plant or tree grows up out of the mud,
*but the flowers and fruits descend. There is a descent as
well as an ascent, and at the point of union there is generation.* This is nature's copulation. Plants, flowers,
fruits, living things, eyes, ears, thought and feeling, do
not ascend out of the ground, no more than the stars or
the sun-light does. There is a mystery connected with
all things which is insoluble, and the ancients deserve as
much respect for their effort to explain it as DARWIN and
HUXLEY.

Man grew, and still grows, as plants and animals do;
but who knows how they come, or from whence? If
thought lies *perdu* in the mind, is it any less an unfathomable mystery, or any less worthy of adoration than if it
be enthroned in the stars or in a GOD? It is just as logical to suppose that sense makes the mind as that mind
evolves sense. In view of these things, I turn to PLATO,
SOCRATES, PYTHAGORAS, GOTTAMA, APPOLONIUS, JESUS,
ZOROASTER, HERMES, MOSES and GOD, for my inspiration. Realizing that inspiration is as potent now as of
old, I ask JESUS and APPOLONIUS if disease and death are
not a delusion of sense. They answer, "They are!"

Far away in the dim and shadowy past some one conceived an idea, and wrote that GOD said: "In the day thou eatest thereof thou shalt surely die." Is it not true? *Is this life?* If so, I do not want more of it! But this is more death than life. The loftiest mind has not yet conceived of real life. This is, indeed, one long-drawn sigh of anguish; a mad dance of demons! A scramble and a rush after toys. If this is life, and all of it, then, indeed, is GOD or NATURE a demon, enacting an awful tragedy, for 'tis worse than a farce. Man dies for lack of vitality; which, indeed, is virility, and virility springs from love, wherein it is generated. So all diseases, pains, and death itself, spring from an abnormal, or unnatural action of love, or the sexual nature. Undoubtedly the ancients understood the "fall of man" to be a *fall of the blood.* The laws of Moses support this conclusion. The rite of circumcision—the rites of purification—the sacrifices with *fire*, and the *shedding* of *blood*, and the obscure narratives of the old Testament show that they considered sin as sexual. The same idea seems to have been entertained by JESUS, for he said: "Woe unto you," etc., "verily I say unto you the *harlots go into the kingdom* before you." Why were harlots named instead of other criminal classes? And again: "Some men are *born* eunuchs; others are made so by men; others make eunuchs of themselves for the kingdom of heaven's sake." This, when rightly understood, does not mean castration. The BUDDHIST priest who has attained the power of "IRDHI, (the power of levitation, of walking upon the water, or of passing through the air, or of visiting at will any of "the three worlds," or "the Brahma Lokas"), has no sexual desires at all, and is as incompetent as an eunuch; but he has all his organs perfect. He has, by a certain course of training, turned his virility upward and inward, instead of allowing it to flow downward, and outward, in the commission of what St. John calls sin. Turn to the first Epistle of John, iii., 9, and you will find the real definition of sin, "Whosoever is born of God doth not commit sin; FOR HIS SEED REMAINETH IN HIM, and he *cannot* sin, because he is born of God." Loss of virility, then, must be sin. Connect this with Gen. iii., 11: "I will put enmity between thee and the woman, and between thy *seed* and her *seed*; it shall bruise thy head, and thou shalt bruise his (?) heel." The word "his" here means *her*. (It has not yet been settled what the serpent here spoken to means. Theology calls it "the devil; but the serpent is the symbol of wisdom). Seed here spoken of must mean the same spoken of by John, for the bruising of it is all too apparent in all the hospitals and medical museums of the world.

Read God's admonition of Cain prior to the murder of Abel: "If thou doest well shalt thou not be accepted? and if thou doest not well *sin lieth at thy door*, and unto thee shall be his desire, and thou shalt rule over him." Strange language to use in order to deter one from doing wrong, to tell him he should become ruler by sinning. "Onan" was slain by the Lord *because sin lay at his door—i. e.*, wasted (Genesis xxxviii., 11). What is a door but a place of egress? Let him who reads think. But we are not dependent upon the Bible and conjecture for what we believe upon this subject. Buddhism, five hundred years older than Christianity, numbering 369,000,000 adherents, containing all the principles that Jesus taught, and much more, teaching the way to supernatural power and "Nirwana," is sexual from the first to last. All birth is sexual, hence "the second birth" spoken of by JESUS must have reference thereto. The curse put upon the woman : " I will greatly multiply thy sorrow and thy *conception*," was a sexual penalty, showing that " the fall " was a fall of the blood ; and as if in corroboration of this idea, nature weeps tears of blood periodically from the mysterious recesses of woman's body. Woman, of all GOD'S creatures, is the only one so accursed. The atonement is of blood and of love. Through woman came the fall, and through the *virgin soul* must come immortality. Salvation is woman's work. By the shattering of the soul into atoms, it lost control of the vital essences, nerve aura, or fire of the body ; hence man *fell* under the control of his passions, and love became inverted. Hence man is the reverse of what he primarily was, and disease takes the place of that divine ecstacy which is his heritage. " The sins of the fathers are visited upon the children to the third and fourth generation." No sins but those of the blood are so visited. Love is the life of the blood, hence in the Scriptures blood typifies love. The blood of the sacrifice of the lamb, and of the atonement, all refer to love. Man's passions are not love, but its lowest expression—its inverted expression. To attain to life and love in its purity the foundations of

GOD'S TEMPLE—man—must not be rotten. If rotten, it must be made new. How Herculean the task ! How gigantic the work ! No wonder JESUS said : "Except a man be born again he cannot see the kingdom of GOD." None but a God could reveal these things of the soul to man ! As I said before, I say again : Meditation is the poising of the wings of the soul for flight, and the most potent meditation is that wherein passions are crucified. Man is an angular being, and in order to attain perfection these angles and triangles must be worn off. Your character and disposition (not your reputation) is indicative of the form of your soul. The man who revolves through life, like a jagged rock—crashing, knocking, bumping, grinding, flaying, and demolishing objects that stand in his way, is far from being a true soul. True, he may get the angles knocked off ere he gets through his journey; but the journey of the soul is infinite, and it takes countless ages of experience to round out a soul to a durable and permanent form, and then, when all the angles and corners are chipped off, it may be a very small thing, scarcely possessing any consciousness at all. But whatever its size may be—provided it is not a monad— it retains its form, and in the lapse of time and the increase of consciousness, the dim past becomes more and more vivid and real, till at last all previous stages of existence become a matter of memory. In whatever form it may be imprisoned, the character manifested will be harmonious and peaceful. The true rounding off of angles is done by the chisel of thought from within. We are the architects of our own selves. We build by our thoughts and acts the temples or hovels we inhabit. Some, indeed, live in caverns, or, reptile-like, in holes in the ground. Some inhabit the great deep, and lie in the slime at its bottom. Soul orbits differ as the orbits of the planets; hence the ages of souls are not alike. Some revolve in small orbits; they make a revolution with great rapidity. Others, again, revolve in orbits so vast that millions of ages are as a second of time, or a degree of distance as from one universe to another. Stations there are on the way of the soul, where rest is taken, and new forms made; mysteries explored; other laws learned, and the soul enlarged. There is no end save to weakness; universe after universe stretches away illimitable. Sense makes boundaries; but soul overleaps or breaks down all barriers. A mere creature here! A nothing, to be scoffed at, doubted, and destroyed by sin, it becomes in its flight stronger and stronger, larger and larger, till it becomes a creator and governor of worlds, and the architect of universes and of other souls. We are merely halted here on our eternal voyage to learn of this peculiar nature—to master its secrets and mysteries. When we have done so, we will go on our way. Some souls are older than others; but no soul can leave this earth unfledged. You cannot leave till you have learned all that is to be known of it, and mastered all its creative forces and laws. True, we have a rest occasionally, of a few thousand years, in some of the heavens or hells of spirit-land or the God-worlds, from which return is not only possible but certain; not merely to communicate, but to be re-incarnated. We sometimes leave our bodies

in deep sleep, and visit strange places, see strange faces,
and learn many new things, which we bring back in part
to our waking state. Waking state ? Indeed ! The real
waking, conscious, living state is when this physical is in
a deeper sleep than the deepest trance. The more globular the soul is, the more easily it may detach itself from
the atoms first, and then and lastly from the body. This
detaching is a drawing together, or contraction, or abstraction of itself, in which is health.

Sleep is better than medicine. The cause of disease is
the close relation, or contact of the soul to the atoms of
the body. The withdrawal of the soul permits the *spirit*
to enter any diseased part and restore it. The soul is
foreign to nature, and its imprisonment therein corrupts
nature. It abhors nature as much as nature abhors it, and
it is bound to get out of it, in one way or another—either
by growth or decay, or by both. From my boyhood I
studied and practiced phrenology, and studied myself
closely. Wishing to make the most of a defective organization, I strove to cultivate myself to the utmost of my
abilities. But knowing my many defects, I felt often dis-
couraged and dissatisfied with myself. One night, in
deep sleep, I was outside of my body. There it lay before me, a mere lump of plastic clay. I said: Oh, you
defective thing ! If I had had the making of you, I
would have made that head far different. A voice said :
" Fix it over to suit yourself." I immediately went to
work upon the plastic head, and moulded it to my notion,
and then got into my body and tried it on. It did not
suit me. Again, I got out and remodeled it, with the

same result. Time after time I essayed to make it over to my notion, but without success, till at last the head was all out of shape; in fact, it was no longer human. And the joke of it was that I could not get it back to its original shape. In my perplexity the voice said: "Trust in creative power! Make the best use you can of your head, and by and by you will have a better one." Then I awoke, and since then I am content to work and wait in harmony with nature, and not find fault. Some of us, at least, are double at times. Nature is not partial to individuals. The way to power is open to all. "Many are called, but few are chosen!" Why? because few *choose* to struggle up the stream, when it is so easy to float, like drift-wood, downward.

To crucify the loves is a superhuman task, and so repugnant to man's everyday life and thought that most men will turn aside from my book in disgust and contempt; and yet there is so much talk in the churches about "taking up the cross!" Alas for unbelief! Whence comes the celibacy of the Catholic priesthood; the asceticism of India, and the peculiar tenets of the Essenes?—amongst whom, it is said, Jesus was "developed." They did not marry, and held property in common, as did the early Christians. They held, as we of the Rose Cross hold to-day, that marriage, *as now understood and practiced* is unnatural. The asceticism of Catholicism, if it was not borrowed from Buddhism, is synonymous with it, which existed long before Gottama's time, who lived five hundred years before Christ. But no matter how old asceticism may be, or how much it

may have been practiced, or how much spiritual power
may be attained thereby, it is the exoteric of religious
ideas, as much so as any of the forms and ceremonies.
The esoteric has never been, and never *will be, given* to
any but the initiated. It is the much-talked-of "PHIL-
OSOPHER'S STONE," and "ELIXIR OF LIFE"—the least of
all known. This subject, however tedious it may be,
is intimately connected with the soul, for it is the SOUL
OF ROSICRUCIA, as well as all religious systems. It is not
asceticism which gives purity—it is only a method for its
attainment. It is from the thought that all things come.
"Not that which goeth in at the mouth defileth a man,
but that which goeth out." Sin defiles, for it "layeth at
the door." The greatest sin a man can commit is the
waste of the life a good and beneficent Creator has given
him for his use, and not abuse. Promiscuity is a mockery
of GOD. The awful diseases that spring from it show the
nature of the sin committed—its *defilement*, and its curse
As the very ground withholds its rest, peace and strength
from a murderer—as GOD said it should from CAIN—so
woman withholds her spirit from the debaucher.

The painful or pleasurable action of any part of the system is due to the presence of the soul in that part. If the
soul be withdrawn from any part, that part has no sensation, and the spirit, taking the place of the absent soul,
builds anew the part afflicted. If the spirit be overcome
by a strong magnetizer, and the soul thus driven back, repelled or forced out, the body has no sensation, and am-
putation or other painful surgical operations may be performed without the subject being aware of it. This fact is

well authenticated. This power of withdrawal of the soul resides in every one who has a will. It does not depend upon the magnetizer at all, but upon the well-regulated action of the will. Self-magnetization is a well-known fact among Spiritualists, and practiced by all mediums to a *certain extent.* But it is too limited to be productive of the results above spoken of. Paralysis is the obstruction—through insulation—of the spirit in its free passage through the system. The soul is left alone in a paralyzed body or limb, without the spirit to give life and power—as all power depends upon movements of spirit, which is effected by its union with the soul. Body is merely the connecting link between the two. The partial withdrawal of the soul is indicated by vibratory motions in the nerves, which, being extended, produces ecstacy, then trance, or insensibility. Those who follow sitting in circles are aware of this.

XII.—MIGRATION AND TRANSMIGRATION.

I have already spoken of progression and retrogression, as balancing each other in motion. The symbol of the Cross in a circle is illustrative of this. The upright, or " Phallus," indicates the law of progress ; the horizontal line the *cross of the law*—retrogression, or the fall of man ; while the circle is the sigma of eternity, or of revolution. Man, in growth and decay, is simply matter in motion, and he must conform to the laws of motion ; *i. e.*, he revolves in an orbit, as worlds do. All life is one ; man differs from the animals only in form and the amount of life and mind he embodies. Life has no beginning nor end ; but forms begin, grow, decay, and end. The law that governs one form governs all. Forms are not progressive to any great extent, but mind is. Consciousness is the highest manifestation of life. Man and animals both exist after death, for power cannot die. It takes ages for matter to progress up to a form perfect enough to manifest consciousness and thought ; so it takes ages for it to retrograde to a loss of it. Even form does not change suddenly ; death itself is powerless to effect any material change in the form ; but the rough garment of the soul merely is cast aside by death, and the spiritual body is immediately formed—fashioned in the mould of the mortal body. But this body, being like the natural body, composed of spirit condensed, is subject to the law of vastation in the spiritual worlds, the same as here. Consequently the form changes, as the soul comes nearer and nearer to the surface of the body. As a man is here, so he will commence on the other side. If he is progressive here, he continues to progress till the merit he has acquired in this life is exhausted, then he will commence retrograding. If he is retrograding here, he will continue on the other side, till he reaches, in the lapse of ages, perhaps, a state of unconsciousness in which he is re-incarnated in some other form. Life is like the revolutions of a wheel; or as the succession of the seasons; or as day and night. There is no such thing as existence without change; and change is alternation, as a rising up and a falling down; though in cycles both vast and small. Repugnant as these ideas may be to modern taste, they are certainly based in logic; and if age gives any prestige to anything, this must take the precedent, for the transmigration of the soul is the oldest religion known to man. Upon the tombs of ancient Egypt there is sculptured in the rock a picture of OSIRIS seated on a throne, and human beings ascending upon a stairway to him. In front of him they seem to divide. Those on the right still retain the human form, but those on the left are animals. Furthermore, there are more people in existence who entertain this belief than otherwise. If you read our Bible, you will see that the JEWS believed in it; and JESUS also. (Mark ix., 11, 12, 13.) Also see Matthew xvii., 10, 11, 12, 13, and xvi., 13, 14; also xiv., 2, 3. Now, for the logic of it : An eternal existence, based upon the pleasure of a *changeable* GOD, is too absurd to think of, but all Christendom holds to such a view. A beginning proves an end. This we show to be an illusion of sense ; for a beginning is only apparently so as regards the life, while it is really so in reference to the form. You had an existence as an infant, but no recollection of it. You also existed in utero, but the mode of that existence was altogether different from life since your birth. You also had an existence as a spermatozoa, and swam around in a drop of semen as a whale does in the ocean, and fought with and destroyed other spermatozoa weaker than your-self. It took a microscope to see you then, but you were a conscious, living being, having the power of volition. Beyond this, science cannot follow you. But we can reasonably believe that you existed in an unconscious state in your father's veins ; and who can know you were not conscious even then ? Shall we assume to deny it, because, in our ignorance, we are unable to find you ? Is not the air full of infinitesimal life, that we know no-thing of ? We know that you, as a spermatozoa, died in the womb before you became a child. Who knows that you had not just died before you became a spermatozoa ? And who knows but that you might have been butchered, as a lamb, a little while before ? What is all this life for which swarms in the air, and walks upon the land, or swims in the sea ? Was it created as a mere pastime for man's benefit ? Or, is it not more reasonable to think that it is all rushing upward towards pefection ?—the fit-test going up and the unfit going down. DARWIN shows the law of "*Natural* Selection." Man! proud and haughty egotist that thou art, Nature thinks as much of a mosquito as she does of you! You gestate in water the same, and go out of life in like manner as a mosquito does. But you make a greater fuss about it. Arogate nothing to yourself because you are a little higher than the poor, patient, dumb brute you drive. Treat them kindly, for you know not how soon they may become human, and pay you in your own coin for your brutality. "Thou shalt not kill," was written upon MOUNT SINAI by one who knew what he was about. The RAHATS of BUDDHISM are not allowed to knowingly tread upon a worm, or to take any life whatever. We are all related, and anon change places with each other in the revolutions of the great wheel of Infinite Power. We know not the effects of violence and bloodshed upon ourselves and others. Note the changes of form and feature from infancy to old age, and see how many times the IDENTITY is lost in a few short years—lost to all save yourself and those in constant association. The slowness of the change makes no difference in fact. How often is it said of one returned after an absence of a few years, "Why, how you have changed! I hardly know you!" Think you those changes will cease at death? I do not.

It is the desire of every man who believes in immortality, to retain consciousness and identity. We are rather in hopes that we will lose some traits—those which we despise; but we would scarcely desire to be something else after death, unless we could be more GOD-LIKE. This much-talked-of identity is but little understood. I am not

the same person I was forty years ago, no more than one
wave on the ocean remains the same till it is beaten upon
the shore.   As wave flows into wave, so life passes into
forms of matter.   A ripple here and a wave there ; a tempest here and a calm there.   Such is life !   The great
wave sinks into the small one, or rises into the large one ;
but whether great or small, the calm levels all.   The soul
has power to identify itself according to its consciousness
of what it has been.   It identifies itself in many ways, by
looks, acts, or by the narration of incidents fresh in the
memory of both.   But if memory is lost and the form has
changed, what good is there in identification, even were it
possible ? which it is not.   I *feel* that I am the same *being*
I formerly was, because I remember the long ago—there
has been one continuous chain of events that have gradually borne me along—there has been no great shock or
disconnection of the current ; but a shock sometimes inter-
rupts the continuity of things. Especially is this true in regard to memory.   The most valuable things are the easiest
disturbed and destroyed—*as we understand destruction.*
How weak, and yet how subtile and strong is memory !
   The past, with its multitudinous experiences, sights, acts,
sounds, etc., fails to keep along with us.   They drop out
by the way, as one wearied falls down to rest, and we look
around at the end of the journey for the companions of
the way, and are surprised at the smallness of the number we see.   And even those that keep the closest to us
are the hideous ones we would most gladly have left behind.   Perhaps we have taken extra pains to outrun or to
evade some of them—but memory drags them along with

almost supernatural power. The greater part of our life is made up of indifferent acts of which we take no note, and which make little or no impression on memory's page, but the great events stamp themselves ineffaceably upon the soul. Memory being, then, the means whereby existence *continues in the consciousness*, its culture becomes of paramount importance, as regards identification. Memory is the soul of genius. We do not know but that the thoughts of the mind are half forgotten memories of previous existences! And *Intuition* may be but a perception of the past and future, in which we have always been as now. Our past lives are as a half forgotten dream. Some little thing calls it up, as from the deep, more or less vividly to our consciousness. There are some things which destroy memory; so, also, there is a way of cultivating or of increasing its power. The opening of the mind to what has been is culture of memory; the closing of the mind to that which has been is the decay and loss of memory.

Memory is the outward or material part of consciousness, as the body is the outward of mind. Hence, to increase in consciousness and soul-power is to expand the memory or the inmost of mind—*the sensorium. Action is expansive*, but *inaction is contractive.*

Bear in mind, now, that by action I do not mean physical or mental action, but *soul action.* The soul is *the principle* of all existence, and is the cause of all action; but its first action is the evolution of a principle which is the GOVERNING MOTIVE or power of every act. The motive is the life of an act. Motives are dual—good and bad. The absence of a good motive leaves the act deficient of its life or expansive power. Hence, the *absence of good* is the evil, which is contractive. The absence of strength is weakness; of sight, blindness; of intelligence, ignorance, etc. That which increases power is *good*, for it leads up to GOD. Good is the only absoluteness of mind—for, as I said before, it is *our estimate*—which descending into acts related to other acts, becomes a relative good, *i. e.*, partly good and partly evil; for it may be good for some, but evil for others. Good, then, which is the least harmful to others, must be the nearest approach to absoluteness, and thus to the truth. There comes from motives a certain *quality* which they impart to every act; and as acts are graded from low to high, so does quality vary. Now, the good of an act is meritorious, but the evil is not, and it imparts another quality to spirit, called Demerit. For spirit is action; and the *motive* of the *act* is *its spirit*—or the quality thereof. Spirit is graded from the *purest white*, through all grades of color down to the *lowest black*. The darker the spirit the more inert it is, for power resides in spirit according to its color. It is the merit of an act which gives spirit its purity of color, but the demerit of it saddens the color of spirit and thus destroys its buoyancy. Merit is the concentrative power of spirit, for it draws all the colors together as in a focus, or prism of white light, or oneness; but demerit is a downward action towards matter—a scattering or refraction of rays—as of many from one in which colors appear—and power disappears in the falling of it, or in its diffusion. Principle is merit, but the absence of principle is demerit. Now, it is necessary to know what a principle is, in order to a comprehension of this recondite subject. A principle is a union of the two highest mental attributes into one spirit. Thus, LOVE and WILL united are *good*, if they unite in TRUTH, and they cannot unite in anything else ; for that which is false is at variance—as a division. Truth unites, but falsehood dissevers. The soul of merit is the *love* of *truth*, and truth is freedom. Thus is merit expansive of the Soul's consciousness, but contractive of the mind. Demerit springs from a want of love of truth, and is a *disunion* of *love* and *will*, hence, is void of principle. In disunion there are differences, which lead to aggressive acts—or acts against freedom.

Aggression is the soul of demerit. The object or motive of an act gives merit, provided the object be for the good of others. There is merit in all love, of whatever name or nature, and it is this that supports life. But there is demerit in hate and revenge, and all passions which confer no good upon self or upon others, and this it is that shortens life, and makes it a continual agitation, and a death in life.

The expansion of consciousness is due to merit, but the contraction of it to demerit. In the expansion of consciousness the soul transcends mere mind, and one becomes conscious of a truth, even without a reason for it. Thus, the past and future rise up in the mind in symbols, or impresses itself as a sensation or feeling. The spirit-worlds may be reached in this way without trance or objective vision. It is a conscious contact of minds, things and principles. Consciousness meets consciousness in this expansion, and the conditions of any state of being may be known. It is a ready reader of character, motives, capacities, past and future events, etc., etc. But the small consciousness is confined and limited by demerit —it reaches little or nothing beyond itself. Merit is acquired by acts of love; it sets the spirit free. Freedom is life and joy. I am aware that some claim there is no freedom of action, and consequently no merit or demerit therein. But we *know* better.

Now, how, or in what manner does spirit rise or become luminous by merit? The spirit has the power to extract life from all substance or spirit, with which it comes in contact, as it radiates in space from the body, and merit is that which increases this power of absorption or appropriation, while demerit destroys that power. Merit eliminates the *tenacity* or *clingingness* of spirit, by reason of which it is held to the surface of things; thus giving it power to *penetrate* deeper into the inner essence or spirit of substance, and to extract the finer essences thereof. Merit increases the radius of spirit in this manner, and it feeds upon *all* things, for there is no repugnance to any. But whatever it may come in contact with it only takes that which is according to its own quality. Now, every object it meets takes something from the spirit; hence, weakens it. Demerit increases taste and repugnance, and in this manner limits the freedom and radius of spirit, thus compelling it to feed upon "husks," often to its weakness and disease. He who is indifferent gets the good of all, and his spirit is fat. But he who likes and dislikes the most, is poor and lean in spirit. These are basic principles of power and progress. Disease originates in this manner. As the beating of the heart throws the blood to the extremities, so does spirit pour out in the pulsations of will. As blood purifies itself by contact with the air, in like manner is spirit purified by the contact of pure things. "To the pure all things are pure." The more indifferent you are, the purer you are, for to the indifferent all things are alike—one.

No man exists in any condition very long after he is tired of it. The man who is forced to exist passes rapidly out of one mode of existence into another, becoming less and less as the circles narrow to the going out. Demerit is that which compels us to exist—but not with a contin-ual consciousness thereof. To increase in power, and the pleasure it alone can confer, requires effort in the acquisition of merit. Merit prepares the spirit, by giving it buoyancy and elasticity. The future life is similar to this. As we come here by force and go out by force, so we enter spirit-life and pass through it. But death is not a birth, and there is not necessarily a growth there as here. The spirit, being a mortal thing, is often diseased, which, of course, weakens it. The laws of demerit are vindictive, and all debts due under it must be paid, and death is the penalty of violated laws. Now, since the mind violates the law whereby the body becomes diseased, the mind is the thing that must die. Physical death is only typical of the real death of consciousness. There are things that wake not up after death, till they awaken in another form —mosquitoes, for instance. This is death followed by a *birth* into another form, but the form of man containing more spirit and greater consciousness, continues after death. But I am satisfied that many never awaken, or if they do, they remain on the earth hovering around mediums; by this means striving to get back to their old habits and vices—thus sapping the spirits of mortals of vitality. Such have an ephemeral existence, and at last fall asleep, and are again born upon this earth. But there are many who lose not consciousness for a single moment, and who are not aware they are dead till some time after: to such death is not a birth into another form, and scarcely into another existence. It is just upon the confines of another existence *into* which the good walk deeper and deeper, and *out* of which the bad are kept by their own inclinations: not only in this, but in all the starry worlds.

In this world, as well as in all the planet worlds of space, every man must stand upon his own merits, and fall by his own demerits. There is no such thing as the transfer of merit or demerit from one person to another. Merit may be driven wholly out of the spirit, as colors may be washed out of cloth. This is done by the accumulation of demerit. So, also, demerit may be driven out of the spirit in the same manner, by making its colors brighter and brighter, by the accumulation of merit. The reason is simple enough: Spirit is the light of the body —its brilliancy is determined by the merit acquired in some previous existence or succession of existences. The brilliancy of the light may be increased by improving the quality of the oil in the lamp as you replenish it. But no other light, no matter how brilliant it may be, can make yours one whit brighter, by being placed near by. You can only change the quality of your light by effort in the acquisition of merit. A pure spirit can only impart to you as *you render yourself receptive thereto ;* and even then it can only give you the crumbs which fall from its table. But crumbs of spirit are better than mountains of gold, for they are health, power, immortality.

Good acts have an influence upon the body in more ways than one. To do good, because it is easy to do so, is meritorious; but there is much more in a good act done when the inclination is the reverse. An act may be forced out by sympathy—which is good, because sympathy is a result of merit acquired in a previous existence—but it may not have much merit in it as an addition to that previously acquired. An act done without sympathy for the sole purpose of increasing good, without any hope or expectation of a reward, has the highest merit therein. A man does not act thus except from deep and profound meditation upon the true relationship of things. Merit is the substance of the celestial worlds, and he who meditates deeply, attaches himself thereto by the elevation of his spirit, and incorporates it into his spirit according to his acts. Thus, it becomes part and parcel of his body, driving out demerit. In like manner could all diseases be healed, were it not for the demerit of former existences. Demerit must be worked out patiently and slowly. In some cases it takes numerous births in the human form, attended with a constant effort, with the object—to get rid of the succession of existence where there is nothing but an alternation of pleasure and pain constantly before the mind, and an idea to enter upon a state of being altogether out of all comprehension. " He that would save his life shall lose it, and he that would lose his life for my sake (the sake of principle) shall save it."—*Jesus.* To teach the way upward is the object of this book.

Principle is the magnet which holds the man steadily to the polar star of power. Mercy is full of merit, if forgiveness comes from the motive to do good. They that do good because it is easy and natural, have their reward as they go along. But he who does good contrary to his nature, through a mastery of himself, lays up great merit in store for a future life—verily his reward shall be great.

To feed the hungry through pity is good, but to feed them with the reflection that by so doing you will help them in the acquisition of merit is far better. It is better to do kindly acts and say kind words without feeling, than to feel and not say or do. Both are good, but one is greater than the other. A small meritorious act may elevate one to the seventh heaven—but he cannot stay there, for when his oil is burned out he must return for more. He will return of his own accord, for he will be in darkness without merit. This earth is the only place wherein merit can be acquired. A little merit will carry a big load of demerit into heaven, but it cannot remain for want of buoyancy. Every act we do, every thought we think, and every word uttered, affects some one else, and we do not know the extent of its influence. Hence, all creation is bound together in the bonds of sympathy.

This is a result of demerit. The Heavens are fast
anchored to the Hells, and there can be no perfect bliss so
long as one poor soul suffers. A chain is not stronger than
its weakest link.

No one can escape the meshes of sympathy without
cutting all its chords. Is this done by love, think you?
Nay! but by indifference. The love of principle is
indifference towards objects. This is the first and greatest commandment—to LOVE PRINCIPLE! The next is love
all things as you do yourself. This is indifference; for
when one loves a principle with all the intensity of his being,
he has no self-love nor love of anything on GOD's green
earth. Now the only principle in existence is FREEDOM.
Neither POWER, nor GOD, nor SPIRIT are possible without
freedom. Look you at the host of martyrs for Freedom!
They loved principle better than self, wife, children or
friends—they were swallowed up in the love of GOD's
freedom! This is indifference to things. Indifference is
" the door " through which merit descends to man, and
through which souls ascend to GOD.

We are all sunk in a psychologic sleep—the falling into
which was effected by sympathy. Those to whom this
life is the most real, are in its deepest phase. They cannot perceive the illusion of it, nor the ineffable glory of
awakening out of it, and the becoming a spectator of
one's own self and of others. This becoming a spectator is
the stepping out of the illusion, as out of one's self, in
which state things are visible in spirit only, or as another
existence. It is like a peering under the floors of conscious
life, as into a great darkness, wherein things become less

and less distinct; or as a passing through a wall of darkness into a great and indescribable light, and, looking back,
behold things as luminous—involved in will, psychologiz-
ing each other; in which sleep they dance with pleasure
or howl and writhe in anguish, as if in fire. Occasionally one gets tired, and seats himself in some obscure
corner to look on. The GODS seeing him thus meditative,
drop down into the mists of sympathy, thus approaching
him in condition, rack his thought and increase his weariness to dissatisfaction and a great unrest--or to hunger and
thirst after something permanent and real. Have you,
too, reader, become wearied of illusory joys, that slip
through your fingers in the grasping, as a phantom eludes
mortal touch? Become indifferent, then, to the love of
life, and gradually the pain and pleasure of it will pass
out of your recognition. Follow me in the culture of
Will, and learn the way to " the door." Space will not
permit me to dwell upon this theme, prolific as it is.
Volumes might be written, and still the darkness could
no more comprehend the light now than in the olden
time.

XIII.—THE WILL.

———

"Men fail, sicken and die, through feebleness of will."
All the potencies of man reside in the will. To its exercise is due all motions—physical, mental and spiritual.
Will is GOD, and "GOD is a Spirit." Therefore, the will
employed in an act is the spirit thereof, or the motive, or
moving force. Man is the focus of above and below—of
without and within. Hence he is susceptible to influences from each. That some are more open to impressions from within than others, is evident; and the same
is true as regards externals. The will is liable to be led
captive and enslaved by either—aye, to be subjugated
and destroyed! But there is a point where the will is
self-poised and free in its action. As the will is the
spirit of every act, it gives *quality* to acts. There seems
to be a warfare between externals and internals, as to the
possession of the will. How oft do we see it verified,
that "A man convinced against his will, is of the same
opinion still." We act as we like to act—we think as we
like to think. We can see very plainly that which we
like to see, and shut our eyes very closely against that
which we do not like. Evidence has but a feeble effect
upon the will. Evil comes from without—or, rather,
from that which is within being overpowered and capti-
vated by that which is without, or foreign to ourselves;

while the good comes from within, or by the *subjection* of the outer by the inner. The *objectifying* of that which is within is idolatry. The *subjectifying* of objects is the destruction of forms, and the resolving of things back to the original essence or oneness from which they spring. This is the digestion of things in the stomach of the mind, wherein the fire is extracted which illuminates the spirit, and is the greatest good to man, for it opens the eyes of the soul; it glows as a light; it warms as fire; it nourishes as food; gives rest and cheerfulness of mind; enriches the blood; purifies the love, and fortifies the soul.

That which is without is transient, fleeting, changing, and impermanent; but that which is within is durable; and the deepest hidden is the most durable of all. The will is the only thing that approximates absolute freedom, and this is not free because of love. Love is worship, and they who love *objects* are idolaters. We are free to will anything we may fancy, but we are not free to love or accomplish, because we are limited by things foreign to ourselves, which we love or hate, or are indifferent to. Love is worship, but hate is its reflection, as things tangible are a reflection of the intangible. Polytheism and Polygamy are branches of the same tree. In the true rendering they mean the same thing. Polygamy was permitted to the JEWS on account of "the hardness of their hearts." *The love of* GOD *is the love of Woman*—not of WO-MEN. But he who loves any *form* is an idolater—the formless *principle* of production is the feminine of GOD.

It is very difficult to understand the foregoing, save in a sinister light, which is a false light. True love is so far hidden from even the imaginations of men, that an effort to make it known is almost superfluous. That love which is awakened by sight or contact of objects is the dark side—the sinister side—of love. Hence the *reality* is not love; it is simply an appearance. But the love that springs from the contemplation of a principle is unchangeable, if it be a true principle, for it springs from light which is real, as GOD is real. As GOD is light, so the will is light; and the love that is produced by will is immortal, because it is pure. That which springs spontaneously from the earth is the weed, bramble, and fruit, which man tries to improve. So it is with the loves. That which springs from impulse is considered by civilization as a thing needing punishment. We believe in cool, calm judgment and self-control, as better than spontaneity. This coolness and self-poise comes from the exercise of will. All civilization is due to self-control. It follows, then, as a logical sequence, that if it is possible for man to guide and control his loves, it is far better than for him to be led by his blind passions. Furthermore, if it be possible to *create love* by any process whatever, it is far better than otherwise. Hence the command to love, not only one another, but our enemies. Such a command is altogether superfluous, if it is not possible to do so. We know how to destroy and disfigure the fair face of nature; we know how to destroy health and happiness, life and pleasure; but we know very little of the creative forces. We know what it is to have the heart beat quick and tumultuous at the sight of beauty, or at the gentle pressure of the hand, or at the bewitching glance of love-lit eyes; but we know nothing absolutely of a power to feel anything but disgust at a loathsome object. Yet it is within the range of human possibilities to love that which to ordinary minds is repulsive—in fact, to love all, and despise nothing. It is the despising of things that separates us from GOD or the SUPERNATURAL. The first lesson in life is the exercise of Will. We learn to use the muscles, but mental effort *precedes* it. The first effort is a projection of power into the nerves, which tremble and go astray of the object the infant tries hard to grasp; but with practice the nerves become steady, and the infant learns gradually to manipulate matter—first, in its own body; secondly, outside of itself. This power comes to the infant out of nothing, as it were, as characters written upon a blank page—nothing—called out into this world of sense by a display of trinkets, colors, sonnets and toys, to be a *something* manifesting power, force and will. The basic principle of all power and of all development is the will. It is all. Every faculty of the mind, every nerve of the body, centres in it. It is the trunk of the tree of life: all else of man are outgrowths of it. Hence the development of manhood begins and ends in the will. It is the centre-stance of being, from which " the rib " of circumstances was taken (or grew), as EVE from ADAM. Will is the first manifestation of soul, or the first faculty it creates for its use.

The will is the great pulsating heart of the Soul—the reservoir of the spirit—which, in its contraction, throws the spirit from itself, and in its opening draws it back again. In the supernatural, the will produces, guides and controls the loves, but in the natural (so called) the loves control and guide the will. Naturally, love is a spontaneous emotion, produced by an object of attraction, leading the will captive. But supernaturally love is an emotion forced out by constant, persistent thought of an Ideal, which Ideal is the feminine *counterpart* of the man, dwelling *within* him, united to him, absolutely inseparable from him. But he cannot have this Ideal in his consciousness, till, in the purity of his spirit, he rises up to its conception mentally. This is a revelation to him, sometimes in early life, but often in age, forced out by unrequited love, and the burning anguish of dead joys. Thus, man becomes dual in his nature first, afterwards in actual marriage with his Ideal, or love.

This Ideal is seldom incarnated on this earth, at the same time the man is; if it ever does so happen, no condition can keep them apart. When they meet, they intuitively know each other. This is marriage in its divine significance. Man and woman thus united by the "Holy Spirit" is eternal—but considered separately they are not eternal entities, but are interchangeable, *i. e.* man is liable to become a woman, and woman is liable to become a man in some other birth. The man hater and the woman hater change places after two or three revolutions of the wheel of life. Human progress depends, then, upon will-culture—and the field to be cultivated is the loves, in

which and from which all things grow. The will viewed
as a mental faculty has its *antagonist*, which is REVERENCE.

Once upon a time when intensely musing upon the an-
tagonisms of the brain, I fell asleep—but it was not all
sleep—when some one came to me, as "the stranger"
came with the mirror. I did not see him, but he showed
me a book. Opening it, he showed me this strange sentence: "The will is antagonized by reverence! In the
foretime the GODS, out of fear of man's ambition, created
reverence." I desired to take the book, but he would
not permit me, but showed me many blank pages therein,
saying: "not now." It was several years before I could
accept the strange dogma. But it is true. We are taught
that the will must be broken in early childhood, and in
order to the salvation of the soul. The opposite is the
truth. GOD does not love slaves nor cowards, and the
child whose will is broken is of no earthly account.

The loves must be tamed—broken, if necessary, by the
will—guided by an *enlightened understanding*. All will
is pure power, and should be increased instead of being
broken. In meditation there is strength, but in reverence
there is weakness—a tacit acknowledgment of a superior.
There is a GOD! nay, many, but if they are superior to
you it is your own fault. You may have been a GOD
yourself at some time, and you may be again with proper
effort. That proper effort is not in humiliation. The
will is represented in the mind as triune, having three faculties through which it manifests itself, as follows:

I.   Firmness—Determination—Stability.

II. Self-esteem—Independence—Self-poise.

III. Continuity—Tenacity—Continuativeness.

A proper balance and harmony of these three constitute a perfect will. The weakness or excessive development of either one weakens the will. As intimated above, an *enlightened understanding* is the only true guide for the will. This enlightenment is illumination of the mind —clairvoyance. There are many degrees of lucidity, but the highest degree is the perception of principles—of " principalities and powers." The inmost and the outermost of being is connected by the imagination. It stands between the will and the loves; hence, all the operations of the will must be through the imagination. It is the " magic mirror " of the mind, through which the soul scans the horizon, or upon which the universe may be made to impinge—not in vague and shadowy forms, many-colored or kaleidoscopic, but in *reality*, either black or white. It is prolific; for herefrom comes all of art, science, literature and beauty, as well as the horrible, grotesque and sinister. Crimes are brooded over and hatched here in the imagination. In this fairy land is death enthroned, for that which is born is the death of something else. This is magic ground from which things grow by the conjuring of the will. Here things dissolve themselves and expose their deformities; and here hideous things are enrobed in garbs angelic. Here religion has its stronghold—for in this the GODS show themselves to man. Maligned, abused, scoffed at, the jeer and laughter-provoking thing yet rules the world. Disrobe man of the imagination and what is he? A brute—worse than savage. His very flesh covers itself with hair, as if to hide its coarseness and vulgarity. But let the imagination loose, and the hair grows soft and fine, or disappears. The flesh glows with fires immortal; the eye loses its savage glare, and man's robes are of the finest texture. The earth, under its rule, is no longer a howling wilderness, but is dotted all over with fairy-like splendors—its magic productions. Steam almost annihilates space, and the lightnings flash thought from pole to pole ahead of old time. This is all due to the dreamings of the imagination.

On the shores of eternity's ocean are greater things waiting for some dreamer to espie and hand down to enrich mankind. All hail to the dreamers, poets, philosophers, preachers, writers and inventors! They have always left their mark, and always will, as an ineffaceable brand upon the face of humanity. Trust, aspiration and hope have their very roots in the imagination. It is only by virtue of it that the good side of humanity in general can be discerned. The unimaginative are the doubtful, unbelieving and distrustful. Have they ever built anything desirable? or ever added anything of value to mankind? THOMAS PAINE was not an unbeliever. He believed in GOD and humanity, and he left his mark upon this people that will be known and felt for long ages. He loved a *principle*, *i. e.*, human liberty, and worked to establish it. PAINE was a dreamer. In his imagination he saw equal rights, and if he lived in this age he would see woman's rights.

Theories lead the van—practice comes slowly along, like a lumbering wagon, afterwards. The imagination is an infinite field. There are many roads in it, and many jungles and angles. All the loves centre here where they impinge upon the will.

"And GOD saw that the *imaginings* of man's heart was continually evil"—*i. e.,* outward. Oh ! that I might impress upon you the vast importance of looking within? May not this be the closet into which CHRIST bade his disciples retire in prayer? What is contemplation but imagination? What is prayer but the aspirations of the soul ? And what are aspirations but images of the soul. How can we "pluck the mote out of our own eyes" in any other way than by looking within? This plucking out of the mote is nothing but the development of clairvoyance—clear seeing. That is done by the imagination. "If thine hand offend thee, cut it off," etc—what is this but the analysis and destruction of passions that retard and hinder the development of the soul to the kingdom of power? If diseases are ever healed by the imagination, is it not a divine gift—better far than medicine? and is it not best to cultivate it? If it will heal the sick ; if it will make life any more pleasant, for GOD's sake let us have more of it.

Three essential elements constitute perfect man, viz : Will, Imagination and Love. These are the positive, negative and neutral. Imagination is the indifferent part of mind, corresponding to indifferent nature—"the door," already explained in previous chapters. It is the "Garden of Eden" out of which man was cast. The same tree of life is there still, guarded by a flaming sword which turns every way.

What more beautiful type of fire than a "flaming sword?" Fire-flame, that guards the way to the tree of life—consuming all impure things that approach the dread portals of the kingdom of power. The pure only are eternal. Purity is original—this is unchangeable. All originality comes to man through *reverie :* this is imagination. Man reaches GOD in .the imagination. In it GOD walks and talks with man. It is the *creative* faculty —not in and of itself, but herein the *will conjures* things from the unknown, and compels them to appear to the consciousness—first, of himself; secondly, of others. In the imagination, things, ideas, passions, hatreds, loves, vices, etc., may be destroyed—first, as realities within; secondly, as obstacles outside of us. For instance, an enemy may be made sick, and gradually to die, or he may be suddenly killed, by the powerful will of an *intensely imaginative* man or woman. Or he may be tamed, subdued, and made a friend of through and by the same power. GOD pity the one who would prostitute such a power to a base or unworthy purpose !

This is hard to believe, but the rationale is very simple to one of comprehension. But it is not my object to teach these things in this work, only so far as to point the road.

There is little power among men on account of the want of will. There is plenty of obstinacy and unreasoning tenacity of purpose. This is due to *firmness,* which is the projecting or repulsive power of will. By the use of it we project ourselves—first, into the nerves and muscles ; secondly, into objects—obstacles that stand in our way. Its work is *outwardly*. We waste our strength and lose ourselves in objects of love, hate, envy and pride. In this projection we leave ourselves *empty*. Emptiness, like filth, invites disease and death. Projection—repulsion—produces death. (*There is a sexual arcana here*: let him who reads ponder well.) We die that others may have being. Firmness is what its name implies—*hardness*. "Firm as the rocks" expresses its real character. It hardens the nerves, muscles and very bones, and also affects the spirit in the same way, rendering it viscid and difficult of motion. That which should be FIRE *emitted* is but a *glutinous mass of molten matter*. Instead of emitting jets of fire, flame-tipped, that reach the soul—the empyrean—the throne of the living GOD— baptizing each other with fire and "the HOLY GHOST," cheering, comforting, exhilarating with divine life and vigor—drawing human souls together in the oneness of a divine love—we emit a force that is like water upon fire —destructive to all real life and happiness—repels man from man, and man from woman, in one universal divorce. Instead of the controlling, persuasive, binding power of will, we have the booming cannon, the dagger and revolver, and the rough-and-tumble fight of dogs.

The "still, small voice" of wisdom is drowned in the deafening roar of countless blood-stained feet, hastening to tread out the wine of human life. In our great marts of commerce, hearts have no more pulsation than the metal that chinks. Firmness—the external of will— hardens everything ! Even human hearts rattle like rocks thrown together. Suppose love to be the only immortal thing : how much will be left of mankind after the fire has removed the impurities of it? Not much! Then roll on your Juggernaut of mammon. Shout and hurrah for kings, priests, popes, bishops, honorables and aristocrats of every grade—your GODS. Dress yourselves in your gaudy shrouds for one universal burial. Marshal your hosts for the grand carnival of death : for what matters the blood of ephemera? Ye pass away like insects! Another race is coming—one in whom this outward tumult of a boisterous will shall give place to silence and peace, and man shall live till he chooses to die. In this reverence—this antagonist of will—all thrones and crowns take root. King-craft, priest-craft and hero-worship must fall together. This vampire trinity fattens upon the best blood of humanity. It makes slaves and minions of the masses. No wonder they all love and preach worship—it is food, raiment and idleness for them, and toil and rags for the human race. It debases mankind, because it robs them of self-respect—the central pivot of the will. The idea that you are beneath another cripples you.

Selfness is nearest the soul—it is the very vitals of will. Confidence in self inspires self-respect. To take away either is like taking off a leg—we must walk on crutches. To feel inferior is to be so. To feel equal is to grow to be such. The proud and arrogant interiorly feel their weakness, and hence arrogate to themselves something foreign, so as to inspire worship in others. The antagonist of self-esteem is love of approbation. This love of the approval of others is one branch of reverence. To be praised and flattered by a king is something grand, and to be coveted. Humble yourself in the dust for a smile of approval from one crowned. To secure the approval of heaven, humble and debase yourself. In other words, act the hypocrite, pretend humility to superiors, but to those beneath you be lord, king, duke or GOD. Such is the effect of modern theological teachings. Self-esteem normally gives the feeling of self-reliance, confidence and independence It gives rise to manly equality and self-poise. It is the balance-wheel, the regulator, the pivot upon which manhood, like a compass, rests.

Self is antagonized by others; hence, he who gives himself up to please others, gives himself to his antagonist—viz : that which ruins him by throwing him out of balance. Be yourself; think yourself; learn of everything and of everybody; be worthy of your own self-respect: for when you have secured that, the respect of others is certain. Be independent, but, in so doing, remember the rights of others. Rights are equal; wrongs make inequalities. If you have any selfhood, consult that first of all. Secure in self-respect, you need not fear others, for GOD approves of self-honor. This is the only glory, and the only way to glorify GOD.

Praise is a false wind—it blows no good. Fame !— what is it, but a breath, shouting huzzas which, prolonged, die away in a hiss ? Breath of the rabble ! the unthinking herd ! One minute exalting you to heaven, the next trampling you in filth. And yet it is said GOD loves praise. The absurdity is too apparent. We cannot add anything to the Infinite. We can, however, join the

Infinite to ourselves, and we are glorified thereby. This it is to "GLORIFY GOD in these bodies, which are His"— or ours in the glorifying. Thus we increase the self-hood—the foundation of all power—will.

Inordinate self-esteem may have no self-respect at all. Self-respect is based in right, truth and justice. Hence, he who respects others and their rights, has self-respect. He who has no regard for the rights of others, although he may possess a powerful *external* will, has a weak will interiorly. He is like a tree with a large top, but whose trunk is rotten. Respect is the very foundation of love; hence, self-respect leads to self-love or egotism. This is an excessive growth from a fruitful soil. Such need pruning. The will, like everything else in nature, grows outwardly to the weakening of its roots. Egotism is the fatal tendency of all aspirations. It is a weakness that must be guarded against. Self-approbation springs from the same source as love of the approval of others—viz: reverence. There is such a thing as self-worship. Egotism is to the will what the moss is to trees in "the sunny South"—it dwarfs and finally kills. Strip man of pretense and egotism (which is the same) and what is there left of him? He who is puffed up and loaded with self-complacency and pride is rotten within. Self-gratification is the root of human action. As we grow we send out many branches, but self-gratification supports them all. No matter what pursuit we follow, or what course in life we pursue, that is the prime motive power. The will is made a slave to it. It is the fundamental principle of all religious systems. The so-called kingdom of heaven is based

in it, and hell is filled with the devotees of self-gratification. Even Buddhism, which claims that there is no
self or Ego in reality, holds out the inducement to its
votaries of escaping to NIRWANA, from the ceaseless and
eternal succession of existences. To this end the senses
are attacked, and bodily or physical and mental gratification destroyed, in order to arrive at the gates of
ecstacy and power—in order *to cease to be.**

So, self is the basis of all, and the only GOD. Pleasure
is the object of all, no matter what road is taken. Even
the materialist finds his pleasure in the quiescence and the
quintescence of matter. Men get religion through fear of
the pains of HELL, and in hope of the pleasures of HEAVEN.
The Hindoo mother tosses her babe into the murky
waters of the GANGES to appease the wrath of her GODS—
in hopes of a reward. The FAKIR of INDIA puts a hook
in the quivering flesh of his back and suspends himself
for days in mid-air, or stands with hands clasped, in one
position, till the limbs are paralyzed, and the finger-nails
grow through the palms of the hands, like claws—all in
hope of power and pleasure other than that of the earthly
senses.

Some seek the ultimate of life in the carnival of carnal
passions, others in mammon worship, others in GOVERN-
MENT POSITIONS, POLITICS, etc. Is all this universal
hunger and thirst—this deathless longing—a mere hallu-
cination? or, is it the index finger of Fate pointing to a

---

* This is the exoteric of Buddhism: the esoteric has never been written.
HARDY translates their sacred books, but frankly admits that if NIRWANA does
not mean annihilation, he does not know what its meaning is.

great truth? Is self capable of becoming infinite in power and pleasure—in this universal changing of conditions and polarities? We of the old school of thought say, Yes.

Of all the potencies of nature, the I, the Ego, the self, is the only thing beyond comprehension that has a positive and tangible existence. All things else are mere appendages of it. I speak of my soul, mind, spirit and body as of my coat, or any other property. But when I speak of myself—of "the think" and "the feel,"—I am at a loss for a definition. To go behind, beyond, above or below myself is impossible. I confront myself at every turn. It is as easy to comprehend GOD as myself, for the simple reason that I and the numeral one (1), are identically the same. One (1) is the foundation of mathematics, from which all numerals flow forth (arbitrarily and absurdly). In the beginning was one (1) GOD, one law, one will. From will came many ones by emission, or emanation. One thing *cannot be added to another*, save by fusion, and even then numbers disappear in the universal one. Add one grain of corn to another; true, the figure 2 represents the number, for convenience, but the addition is arbitrary—there they remain, separate and alone, each an individual thing. In nature there is no addition. Fusion and emanation are the only mathematical laws. Division is as arbitrary as addition. Divide a grain of corn and it loses its individuality. Plant the grain and it emits from itself whole ship-loads, but it loses itself in so doing. Now GOD emanated from Himself all things, which, in the beginning, were as like Him as one thing can be like another. Perfect man was the first emanation. He existed long before this world or any of the lower orders had an existence. He (man) was all in himself—*i. e.,* he was the first or great primal law of creation. Laws are modes of action: man is an action of GOD or WILL. From man's will flowed all lesser laws or things. The Ego, the I, myself, is an emanation of GOD—a creative action—the first and the last and the whole—(1). The lower orders are man's creations—degenerated human beings, lesser things, laws or acts. The sage of Genesis simply got the cart before the horse when he said the animals were created before man. Afterwards, however, he rectifies the mistake partly, when he speaks of the "Sons of GOD" marrying the daughters of men. These "Sons of GOD" were the primitive men, of which I have spoken. I am the creator of all my acts—they are laws. They flow out through effort of will—being projections of the Ego—myself. Thus GOD *meets man—is man—in the selfhood.* The selfhood is GOD humanized. The selfhood of animals is GOD brutalized. We can understand how it is possible for man to produce that which is inferior to himself, but it is more difficult to conceive of his creating anything superior. How can the animal evolve man, who is *superior* in every essential? How can man progress unless there is something above him to which he is near related? This relation is found in the self hood—the central pivot of WILL. Be very careful, then, reader, how you trifle with yourself. Every thought and act which debases you, *i. e.,* sinks you in your *own inner consciousness,* that which

you wish to hide away in some dark corner of yourself—
away from the eye of even yourself—debases GOD. The
day comes speedily when he will sit in judgment upon
your every thought and act—and that upon the throne of
your own conscious self hood. Firmness is the moving
force or controlling power of this outward sensuous life—
the power of aggression, of overcoming obstacles by physical force. It is the masculine of will.

Self is neutral—hermaphrodite—neither masculine nor
feminine. The feminine of will is represented by CON-
TINUITY. Self-esteem, phrenologically, is located just
above the crown of the head ; firmness, a little in front
or above it, at the highest point of the cranium ; while
CONTINUITY is just below self-esteem—inferior in position
and diminutive in size, situated just above the social
group, as a mother keeping guard over her children.

Understand, that the will is a trinity. One part does
not act without the co-operation of the others ; they are
inseparable. For the sake of illustration and analysis,
and to make comprehensible that which follows under the
head of will-culture, and to show the rationale—or the
modus operandi—of creative power, these distinctions are
made.

The feminine is the attractive, and hence, the *productive*
principle of nature—that principle which collects matter
and combines it into forms. The principal office of continuity is the drawing of the spirit together—to a focus—
preparatory to *projection*. There is always a concentration of force or energy in all effort, and the greater
the concentration the greater will be the power mani-

fested. The tension of the nerves and muscles is due to continuity—oneness of force and energy. It lays hold, as with hands, of each mental fibre, and guides the fiery steeds of spirit. Spirit obeys mind, but mind is under the will. Continuity is intenseness—*continuativeness*. Once directed to an object, it fastens itself to the spirit thereof, and, leech-like, sucks its very life out. If continuity be large, one becomes absorbed in any pursuit, object or passion, to the *forgetfulness* of other things. It *cannot* let go. This leads to insanity, which is simply the unbalancing of the will. Consciousness is a result of the poising or *posing* of the will: hence the polarization of the will is the true work of him who aspires to infinite conscious power. The will oscillates, similar to the needle of a compass, or the balance-wheel of a watch, or as a beam very nicely poised. Too much attraction in any given direction, or too much weight at one end of the scale, causes change of polarities, which is a change in the conscious life of thought, memory, feeling or sensation. When this change is extreme, the being is changed, the memory is lost, or judgment is dethroned, and yet the form of the being remains apparently the same; but the man himself has vacated his throne and become a servant of some other power greater than he. In view of this philosophical truth, we claim that there is no real sanity on this earth, and very little of it in spirit-life, beneath the abode of the GODS. There are no perfect wills. Either firmness, continuity or self-esteem are too weak or too strong for proper balance and harmony. In this mundane sphere the masculine weighs down the

feminine, and, worse even than all that, the central dia-
mond of the soul—self hood—is marred and corroded till
there is no perfect oscillation or movement. We have
moved, like a wagon, so long in one rut that it is almost
impossible to get out of it. We have looked so long at
the *black side* of GOD's sign-board—nature—that it has
become luminous to us ; and at the white side—spirit—so
little that it has lost its lustre and is forgotten, or, supposed at most to be the night of nothingness. This is
insanity. A man may be insane in whole or in part : in
either case, the will, becoming unbalanced, has lost control in whole or in part. It has lost its grasp. The
reversal of the poles of the will is why we have no memory
of previous states of existence. The will, by chance,
accident, sickness, or by intent, may oscillate back to the
point it occupied in some former age, or previous state
of being, and the person be exactly what he was spiritually at that time, and lose all memory of this life. A
psychologized person may be made to feel and act like a
dog, while under the influence. Why ? Just because his
will is thrown out of balance, and he is what we call, in
other circumstances, insane. It is just such effects that we
call insanity. In all similar cases of insanity where the
psychologist is not seen or known, it is the spirit of some
one unknown, either mortal or a spirit. At such times we
say he is insane. The consciousness of being remains, but
memory—the bridge over the chasms of time—is broken
down, but not totally destroyed. It may, however, be
reconstructed by the culture of the will, and all remem-
brances revived. Continuity is that power which leads to

forgetfulness of these surroundings—to abstraction and absorption. It is when we become absorbed in some work or passion that we forget our weakness, or what we know of ourselves, and rise up to grandeur and glory. The greatest achievements, the most heroic deeds, the greatest discoveries that bless mankind, are all due to this little feminine faculty of will, which leads to insanity. The diffusion of spirit, the waste of life, the weakness and misdirection of energy, uncontrollable passions, the want of psychological power, the pains and aches of the body—these are all due to the weakness of continuity, and excessive self-consciousness. This self-consciousness is a rut dug deep by demerit, in which we are all sunk—as in a quagmire. Purity of self is the only help for us—the only lubricator of the will—the only cleanser of this human time-piece. Purity—physical, mental and spiritual—cannot be achieved by outward acts. It is an inward effort—an inward fire kindled by the action of continuity, which burns out the dross of these gross natures. This fire is kindled by the *accumulation of spirit whenever and wherever attraction overbalances repulsion.*

The great majority of our acts are involuntary. Even
the acts which we think we do voluntarily are mainly either
forced or coaxed out of us by an impulse. But, no matter how this may be, we know we have volition, or voluntary powers, however small they may be ; or no matter
how vast the involuntary may be, it is subservient to us.
Call it what you like—NATURE or GOD—it is our servant. When once this machine is set in motion, it au-
tomatically obeys. A musician, after he has mastered
the use of his instrument, does not will each separate
motion of his fingers; his mind may be occupied with
words he may be singing to the music, but his fingers
move fast or slow in accord with the music, and his feet
work upon the pedal without attention or thought. So it
is with all we do. In doing a piece of work with which
one is familiar, the thought wanders away, but still the
work goes on. In sleep the voluntary is suspended, *i. e.*,
the mind is at rest ; and at times the will also seems to
rest, or memory and judgment to be suspended.

Habits all become automatic, or involuntary. Habits of
the body and mind are alike, and yet the voluntary seems
to be of the mind : in fact, they are so closely allied, and
so interwoven, that it is difficult to separate them, or to
define them as separate powers. But we do know that all

the light we have is of the mind, and all the power of it comes from the involuntary. Voluntarily we do as we *think* best, but the power to accomplish is the most of it. Thus it seems plain to me that the voluntary powers are merely a thought we have, which thought is all we have to guide us. It is possible that this thought may be so cultivated and enlarged to become as automatic as any habit, and express itself as any involuntary power, even in our sleep.

Language is a mere matter of culture or habit; and so of thought, or any of the bodily functions. Indigestion may be cured; torpid liver made to act; and constipation of the bowels overcome, by paying *constant attention* to regularity. By paying little or no attention to the movement of the bowels, thus breaking up nature's habits, their warnings become less and less, and, in time, habits of constipation or inaction intervene. But if you will have a regular time for the evacuation, and pay strict attention thereto, providing an opportunity, whether there is an inclination or not, nature will in time listen to your demand, and furnish the power to remove all obstructions, and give life to the torpid tissues. Such is the force of habit.

This new life comes through an effort of the will—first, voluntarily, but afterwards as an involuntary power or habit. When it has become habitual, the bowels will notify you of the time, and insist upon your paying attention. It is the same with eating and drinking: if you eat three times daily, you will be hungry at those regular times; but if you have no regular time for eating, hunger

will not come till you think of it. To think of food as
of something loathsome will kill hunger. To break in
upon the regularity of a habit is to destroy it. To pay
attention to anything is to become its slave. Sexual
excesses are habits of thought, depending upon regularity
for existence. So long as it is a habit, it will demand
and enforce attention; but turn the thought to something
else, and the voice of the habit gradually grows weaker
and weaker, till in time it will take an effort of thought
and the conjuring of the will to restore it.

Small as the voluntary powers may be—perhaps a mere
thought, yet it is all there is of us, and our weal and woe
depend upon their use. By use the voluntary becomes
the involuntary. Absentmindedness is indicative of the
sinking of the voluntary into the involuntary. Such persons are more indifferent to outward things than those
who are always "wide-awake." This is, indeed, the
beginning of trance, wherein some of the very finest
orations are delivered.

This "wide-awake" life is a mere habit, which is destroyed by the creation of another, viz: sleep. Sleep is
a closing of the eyes to outward things and the turning
of the sight inward. It is the same in trance: the first is
a sleep, or a partial sleep, of the consciousness; the latter
is a higher degree of consciousness: for the full wakeful-
ness of the soul's powers is in a union of the voluntary
with the involuntary. This is effected by magnetism, and
sometimes in natural sleep; then we have somnambulism,
or sleep-walking, if the soul is unable to quit the body;
but if the soul is able to quit the body, we have prophetic

visions, or the solving of difficult problems, or the visiting of distant places, spirit-worlds, etc. But in whatever way sleep or trance may be induced, it produces a degree of insensibility in the body. The deeper the sleep, the more insensible the body becomes. Mesmeric sleep is next to death. This may be self-induced, or through the agency of an operator. Calmness and tranquility are necessary to its production, the same as in natural sleep. Calmness allows the soul to expand, and this produces sleep and trance, wherein the body becomes insensible. But there are two ways of producing nervous insensibility: one I have described; the other is through increased and intense activity or excitement. Fits, in which sensibility is lost, are produced by excitement—the cause sometimes visible or known (or, at least, supposed to be), but oftener unknown.

We know that catalepsy, common to Methodist revivals, known as " the power," is induced by excitement. Children fall down in fits through the excitement of fear. In intense anger the nerves have little or no feeling. Indeed, there is an insanity comes through anger in which there seems to be no sympathy, reason or feeling. Many a man has been maimed, wounded, and *materially injured* in a fight, and not been the least sensible of it till the excitement was over. So long as the tension of the nerves continues there is no pain. The clenched fist of an angry man feels nothing. The Indian, undergoing untold tortures at the hands of his captors, sings his war-song and laughs in the face of his tormentors. MICHAEL SERVETUS, being roasted on a slow fire made of green wood, by

JOHN CALVIN, composed the following, which he repeated to his tormentor, with a smile of happiness on his face while broiling :

> " This side enough is toasted :
> Turn me, tyrant, and eat ;
> For, whether raw or roasted,
> I am the better meat."

The Christian martyrs while being burned at the stake, sang, prayed and exhorted; assuring the bystanders that it was pleasant "to die for the LORD." In view of these facts, and what we know of ecstacy and the insensibility of the mesmerized subject, is it not at least reasonable to suppose that the will is master of sensation as well as motion ? There is no pain to the strong will. Many a man has endured surgical operations without the use of an anæsthetic, or being bound, and with not a movement in muscle or nerve. Now if pain can be *partially* subdued by the will it may be wholly so. A man is made many times stronger and many times more enduring by excitement ; but the deepest and most power- and health-producing excitement comes from the calming of passions and the awakening of the higher faculties. There is a spiritual excitement, far more potent and exhilarating than the excitement of any of the passions, in which ecstacy is passed and the soul escapes. It is then that these bodies are proof to the elements, and command the respect of even wild beasts. The RAHAT of India seeks some jungle or lonely place, or some dangerous place by the side of some swamp or lagoon, infested by monstrous reptiles, where man fears to intrude; here he composes himself for his meditations, and goes calmly into an unconscious state, and the monsters crawl out and lie down by his side, and sleep also. Never was one known to be harmed by them. (See Isis UNVEILED). Is not this the same power by which DANIEL commanded the respect of the lions in their den ? The full power of the will does not manifest itself in our normal state; there must be an excitement of *some kind* in order to call into play all our powers. But the full measure of power is not in the tension of the nerves and muscles ; it is in the tension of the inner man or spiritual body. This is not a rousing up as of anger, and a propulsion of the spirit outward, but rather a letting go of the nerves—a resignation of the soul as in sleep. This is possible only in habit. True culture gives resignation, which, pushed on to extremes, gives power to withstand fire. The ACOLYTE for the Priesthood of Buddhism must possess supermundane powers ere he can be admitted. I have been told by a gentleman who was born in India, and lived there until he was twenty-one years of age, that they are tested when they apply for Priesthood by being required to walk over a long bed of live coals of fire with their naked feet, and *to do it without hurry*, and to come off at the other end without a singe or smell of fire ; if they fail they are not admitted, but are sent back to their practice of meditative rites. D. D. HOME is one instance of our own time and country who has manifested this power, as well as that of levitation, by virtue of which JESUS walked upon the water. I might multiply facts " *ad infinitum*," if it were the intent of this work. The

past and present are both full of the proof. Search for
it,—not alone in the Scriptures of the olden time, but in
the living testimony of the present. The will is a magical power; but its highest magic is in letting go. The
strong well-balanced man accepts things as they come
with a spirit attuned to the sweet melodies of creative
power: and weeps not over blighted joys or withered
hopes. He looks above and beyond these things, and
his soul is filled with rest thereby. He does not essay to
control others, for he has as much as he can do to control
himself. By this means he converts his enemies into
friends, who come to him, as an oracle, for counsel. His
control is far greater than that of one whose whole life is
spent in trying to control others. The gigantic evils of
this life come from the desire to rule others—or to make
others do as you wish them to do. Counsel is far better
than rule. Let every one do as they like, but scatter
light and knowledge of the true way to happiness and
power. Reader, if you have lost youth and happiness—
let go! If friends have proved false and ungrateful—*let go!*
If your heart is torn by unrequited love—*let go!* If you
are poor—*let go!* If you are wealthy—*let go!* If Providence forsakes you—*let go!* If you love life—*let go!* If
you are tired of life—*let go!* If you look back upon your
life's journey with regrets—*let go!* For " He that would
save his life shall lose it, and he that would lose his life
shall save it."

XV.—WILL–CULTURE.

Let him who aspires to power commence by a close and critical analysis of himself. As will is the *extraordinary* of man, its culture is the culture of the entire man, and the regeneration of him—or another creation. The methods of it will be found as extraordinary as God himself—for how can a thing cultivate itself without God's help? And God's methods are not our methods.

The *three great principles* of the selfhood, from, by and through which all actions come are (1) Love; (2) Imagination; (3) Will. The Imagination is neutral, as indifference or nature; Will is masculine; Love is feminine. As a husbandman must till the soil in order to make it productive, so must a man culture his loves in order to the production of will-power. As a slave must first overcome his master before he can be free, so must the will overcome its loves: hence, love is the way of freedom, of regeneration, and power. Self-analysis shows impurities which must, as a primary step, be removed. There can be no progress without vastation. The old habits, vices, follies, modes of thought, loves, hates, envy, jealousies, covetousness, fear, pride and egotism must all die and be buried far out of sight as a preparatory step to soul-growth; and will is cultivated and made strong in the subduing

of those things which limit its freedom and power.
Purity is the only thing that cannot be destroyed ;
so, the purity of love, will and wisdom are immortal.
It is only the *semblance* of *real things* which die or
change ; hence, that which is supposed to be real love,
or real will, or real wisdom, is only the semblance of the
real, for they change or die. So, in the regeneration ;
the semblance must pass away to give place to the real.
These bodies are mere reflections of ourselves, which we,
seeing in the mirror or mirage of nature, fall in love with,
and embracing, die. Now, this law is the same in relation
to sex-love—we love the reflex of ourselves which we see
in the *mirror*, called woman. This is not real love, for
its operations being downward, we propagate only our
kind, or conditions, or emanations, which are antagonistic
to us ; while real love propagates new atoms—parts of a
divine body, unchangeable and eternal—its operations
are upward, and its emanations mingle in the essence of
GOD.

The infinite is all power, and it is man's field of operation. It encompasses him round about; it bends to him
with anything he asks for ; but we must work for what
we want. "Not every one that saith, Lord ! Lord !
shall enter the Kingdom ; but he that doeth"—*i. e.*, he
that *worketh with a will* in the *right direction*. Now the
road to power is in the perfection of our nature ; which
is in the attainment of duality first. I have already spoken
of ideal love, of its conception, growth and union, or
marriage in the spirit. Now, the true methods of will-
culture have for their object growth. Soul-growth is

inward, or a letting go of outward things, and a looking forward to the realization of a true life in which true love appears as one with the will, or the female united to the male in real durable oneness of being, or marriage. There can be no union of objects; therefore, man and woman, being separated entities, are not one—neither can be—on this earth : hence, marriage is a semblance or type of a *reality*, or changeless condition. A union of two in one, or two in spirit. This will be more fully set forth in the chapter on *Gifts of the Spirit*. Harmony must be first had *in* the individual ere it can be effected with another, and for this reason a lifetime of effort or culture is necessary, in which things inharmonious or at variance with each other are to be avoided. Owing to the inharmonies of marriage (and the loss of power therein) the Essenes and Rosicrucians of old discarded marriage as something unreal, and lived lives of celibacy. For this reason the Buddhistic and Catholic priesthood are not permitted to marry. Further reasons are set forth in regard to the nature of sin, to which the reader is referred. In order to destroy that which retards the soul in its flights, viz : sin, its opposite or antagonist must be strengthened ; to this end the whole mind must be given up to the contemplation of such things as make the soul sick and disgusted with sin. This creates another *emotion* antagonistic to love, viz : feelings of disgust at that which the world is mad after. Love is an *emotion*. Will is *motion*, but love is a *reflex* of it, or an *emotion*, or *wo-man*, because emotions ruin the will or the man in leading it into captivity. The object of love is to join itself to the will in order to increase power to enjoy, as a loving wife works for and delights in the happiness of her husband. So woman should not unite with man save for the purpose of begetting *life, spirit, power*. In true marriage, according to the divine intention of it, there are no children; and no disease; neither do they die. To have an ideal elevated, pure and full of rest and unalloyed pleasure, is to have the pain of disappointment in realization. It is to kindle a consuming fire at your very vitals, which you are obliged to quench by the will, because no heart answers your heart-throbs; because all fall short of your ideal love—this it is for him to suffer who aspires to be something more than the common. There is no greatness not born of pain, and there is no pain greater than that of a heart bruised; so soft is it, and flexible, that it will not break.

Sexual love has the strongest hold of any of the passions; it is the hardest for the will to turn from its lust. The effort to idealize love in the imagination is analogous to that of the libertine and debauchee—only one is chaste while the other is impure. The onanist sees in his imagination the object of his lust, and thus acting upon his emotions pollutes himself. It is the same with the libertine. These emotions that destroy power and the soul are created by an inward action; and in proportion to the power of concentration is the spirit drawn within, condensed and projected, and thus the life, spirit and power thrown away. But this wasted virility, though lost to the man, is not lost in nature, for it is a protoplasm from which spring infusoria, worms, insects, reptiles, etc., which are a curse to the earth and mankind. Your ideal love may not be a very near approach to true love; but your highest conception of womanly beauty, purity, goodness, truth, grace and excellence, coupled with form and action, is *your estimate* of it, and as such is *your* kingdom of power towards which you grow rapidly or slowly as the case may be.

Control must begin at home—*in the selfhood.* But how, or in what manner, can a thing culture and control itself? How can the will regulate its own action? Firstly, then, the will is the nearest approach to freedom of any-thing we know of; love is limited by the sensibilities; wisdom, by that which we learn; but will, being free from emotion, is free to produce emotions according to its love and wisdom. So, love and wisdom are the shackles of the will. *Now, we do not control that which we love; that which we love controls us.* Hence the necessity of subduing love as the beginning of the road to power. We do not destroy love, but we wean it from sensuous objects. Thus weaned, it becomes at one with the will in its freedom, and the flights of the soul. This is the At-one-ment—(Atonement.) Love cannot be purified. "There is no impure love," said P. B. RANDOLPH. What we call purifying love is *merely the vastating of pretences.* Love itself is honest; but this world's love is in pretending to be what we are not. It is the shame, which, in order to hide, GOD clothed ADAM and EVE in the skins of animals. If all the shame were removed from mankind, the little love left would be very small indeed.

Will-culture is a thing altogether antagonistic to gen-

eral religious ideas ; for the will is generally considered of the "evil one"—to be broken and crushed.
With this idea I am at variance. We have far *too little*
power, and to increase in it is the acme of all religion.
It is the false direction of power wherein evil exists, *not
in the power itself.* To enlighten the mind, then, or to
culture the imagination, is to control man's creative
powers or loves, and guide them in the right direction.

All culture must begin at home. Begin by a recon-
struction of *yourself.* If you feel that you are superior to
others, disabuse yourself of that idea at once. In arro-
gance there is no growth of the soul. To feel as you
really are, is to feel very weak and very small. In order
to rise above the common level, you must be *real.* To
feel equal is to feel real and to be real. Let every man
have his opinions in freedom—the rights you claim, freely
grant to others. Thus you pluck the motes out of your
eye. Judge no man, for you know not their motives.
The freedom you claim for yourself, that grant to others,
even in thought and feeling—for freedom is the principle of growth—the first and the last, and the only principle in existence. Now he who is bound by love, hate,
or any passion whatever, is not free. How can he expect
to have power? Power only comes by freedom. To be
free, then, necessitates a *cutting loose* of the bonds of
slavery. To love nothing, to hate nothing, to have no
likes or dislikes, to have no prejudices, no tastes, no
preferences—this it is to be free. The little power we
have comes from freedom. Now let him, who expects to
culture his will, bear in mind this fact—that it cannot be

done for a selfish or mercenary purpose. I am aware that one part of it, viz : firmness and self-esteem may be cultivated and increased, but it is not real culture of the will after all, but a *throwing out of balance* of the will, which is destructive in the main. All power, to be lasting, must *descend* from the higher to the lower, as a baptism ; and this descent is accomplished by and through the feminine of will—viz: Continuity. The second act of will is in the propulsion of force into the nerve—as in grasping of the hand or in the striking of a blow. But the first effort of will is in the *gathering together* of force *before striking.* The latter is an *expansion* act, like the inflation of the lungs ; the former is an exhaustive act, as the expiration of the breath. Now the *first*, or *primal*, or *foundation* of all power is inflation. This is concentration, and involves the exercise of continuity. The greater the concentration, the greater will be the power manifested—either in physical, or in mental, or in spiritual effort. Now, in making a great physical effort, there must be a stimulant or an excitement, in order to a manifestation of the full power of the individual. This excitement, of course, is a mental effort in which the mind expands to its utmost tension of energy, or feeling, or want of feeling, in which a *resolution* is formed, born or begotten, and the nerves and muscles are braced up— filled to overflowing with force. The whole person *expands*, as a prospecitve mother, and is eager to deliver itself of its superabundant force, energy or burden. When full to overflowing with anger, love or any passion, we are eager to express it : but the first effort is to be full.

This is a mental effort in which the *will gets its excitement* from the dwelling upon *wrongs*, or *love*, in *the imagination*. Now, this "brooding" over wrongs, or dwelling in thought upon things involves the exercise of continuity. From this it is known that the real power of will comes from the feminine part of it, viz : concentrativeness or continuity. It is also evident that the more one *believes* in the *reality* of the wrong or love, the fuller they will become of love or anger, and the power of its manifestation will be proportionally greater. Now, this is exactly the case in all occult or spiritual power. The excitement of the will comes from its *dwelling upon an idea or an object to be attained* and in the *resisting of the excitement* of the passions. In fact, the culture of the will is in the alternate excitement of the passions, and in subduing the same without expression. For instance : Some one wrongs you a *little ;* you seize upon it as if it were a sweet and delicious morsel, and by constantly thinking of it in its most aggravating features, and by dwelling upon it, you work yourself into a mental fever in which you feel like "knocking down," "kicking," "shooting" and "dragging out,"—but you do no such thing ; but before your passion is too strong for you, you turn your mind to another feature of the wrong, and begin to look upon it as not *quite* so hideous, after all, and gradually it grows less and less, as the excitement cools down. You have not manifested this to the world, but it has had an effect upon *you.* Your will power has grown in the exercise. Physical power grows by manifestation, but spiritual power, by silently suppressing or repressing it.

If you express your power physically, it is lost to you spiritually. Hence the motto : "Silence is strength." In thus exciting yourself, and then *controlling* yourself, you are creating power, as well as teaching the involuntary powers obedience. After practicing for a while this exercise, you will find you are becoming very excitable, and you can excite yourself even *without* any outward provocation. A jealous person can easily become half crazy about nothing. In this manner you learn how to *create* emotions of a low order first, and then you gradually step up to emotions of a higher order, such as mirth, love, pity, rapture ; but of all creative emotions, that of love transcends all else. To gaze at a dead body with worms crawling in and out, and look at it as human, and think that that is the end of all flesh, and that you will be the same in a short time, disgusts one fearfully with the follies of life, and tames the passions of any man who thinks at all. This helps the will to gain the ascendency ; but after seeing it once or twice, you can see it in your mind at any time, and thus subdue all low and unworthy thoughts and feelings—this strengthens the the will. "He who keeps death in view seldom does a wrong." The will that cannot create emotions by its own effort is weak : it needs a stimulant. To keep your heart young and full of tenderness and love for your companion, think of her as when you wooed and won her. To destroy your love, think of it in connection with something disgusting and low, and it will speedily die ; but do not be deceived ; some things die very hard. Habits take hold of the vitals. Many who read these lines may be able to see what they desire in the mind without physical contact. Such can develop power rapidly. Others, again, will need some aggravating circumstances to stir the emotions. To provoke another to anger with words, looks and gestures, and then subdue yourself with a thought, and control and subdue the other by the creations of mirth or grief is a good exercise, but a dangerous one.

Who can stand and calmly take a blow without resentment? But it was in view of this same subject that JESUS said : "If a man smite you on one cheek, turn the other also." Habits are hereditary as well as acquired. They, like diseases, are hard to cure. All habits of the ordinary man tend outward, and hence are weakening. To be more than ordinary, work against habits. This is done only by creating other and opposite habits. "Does thine eye offend thee, pluck it out !" or train it not to see objects external, by turning it inwardly. Perhaps you are fond of some particular article of diet—you love the taste of it. Pork, for instance. You first satisfy yourself that it feeds scrofula and the humors of the blood, and you desire to leave it off. You go to work to kill the taste for it by becoming disgusted mentally with the thing you delight in. It is done by meditation thus : Imagine a stomach filled with flesh fermenting and working like maggots in carrion. Flesh in the stomach, as in the sun, becomes putrid. It is nothing but a bit of corpse dressed and cooked, that I am eating. Behold the market ! hung round and round with corpses, not unlike my own, if it were dressed like these. A little

while ago they were moving, living beings, like myself.
I know that I become like that upon which I feed. See
the swine! the scavenger of the filth of living things;
what a loathsome object! and I am his scavenger. "I
am naught but a sepulchre full of rotten flesh." Behold
the butcher! A living corpse cutting up dead ones! while
others stand eagerly looking on, with mouths watering
like dogs for the feast of rottenness. See the carts laden
with corpses!—hurrying away to the meat shops—yet
warm with life, holding up their naked, mutilated limbs
in mute appeals to heaven against the horrid butchery!
while a demon in human form, sits driving to the char-
nel house. By such thoughts persisted in, the taste
changes, and the stomach heaves at the sight or thought
which we conjure in regard to food or anything else.
Thought is sight, feeling, tasting, smelling, etc., all in
one. The taste changes, as our thoughts change in
regard to it. Just so with all the passions.

There is no virtue where there is no temptation; no
merit where there is no demerit; no grace where there is
no sin; no power where there are no obstacles. The
greater the obstacle overcome, the greater the glory of
the achievement. The filthiest thing contains the most
life; but this life is worthless till utilized.

The will is the husbandman, who, if needs be, drains
his ground, enriches, plows, harrows, plants and cultivates his crop. If he be not slothful, he shall, according
to nature's laws, reap his harvest. So with the aspirant
to power; he must prepare his body, his blood must be
filtered, and the acids and alkalis harmonized, and the

flesh made soft, sweet and glowing. Drugs will not do this. The body must be reached through the mind, or not at all. It is a well-known fact that the imagination affects the body. Fear, disgust, and in fact, all the passions have an effect upon the blood. One may accelerate the action of the heart, while another retards it. All the passions get their excitement from the imagination. So, the imagination is the connecting link between the body and the soul. It is the door between the visible and the invisible worlds of sense. To purify the body, then, the will must affect it through the imagination. The imagination corrupts the blood ; why may it not purify it as well ? That we do not know how this is done is no argument against this proposition. Love tinges the cheek with the glow of magnetic health ; fear congeals the blood ; disgust produces neuralgia, and lust produces consumption. Hate dries up and coagulates the humors ; covetousness produces dyspepsia,—and so on to the end of the chapter.

Every passion, and even thought and reason have their roots in the imagination. The effect that things have upon us depends upon the way they are looked at. Beauty and deformity spring alike from the imagination. We receive the spirit of a thing by looking at it—smelling, tasting, hearing—and more than all, by thinking of it. We get the grossness of food by eating it, but the real life of it is extracted by the thoughts we have of it. In other words, the ideas we have in regard to the quality and use of food imparts to it something akin to themselves.

Thus the body may be gradually changed by diet ;

not so much by quality as by quantity; for the will *imparts any desired quality*. A very sensitive person suffers nausea by the sight of *that* which is loathsome— to conjure that thing up in the *imagination* has the same effect. Many a person is afflicted with dyspepsia and other disorders from a settled conviction of the inevitableness of it. The idea that you *will cure yourself* is better than medicine. The idea that you will eat simply because you are obliged to do so in order to live, *and not for the pleasure of eating*, is better in reality than food or fasting; but to eat, drink and love for the sole object of attaining immortal power, and not for the sensuous gratification of the appetites or passions, is to work upon the mind, blood, body and spirit as GOD works—downward. This downward operation eliminates the grossness, and leaves the essences or life for your use. Remember this simple thing : *All impurities are a result of compounding, or of combining different substances, fluids, magnetisms and spirits in one.* Purity is oneness. The simpler the diet the better ; one thing is better than three, four, or a dozen. Never eat for pleasure, and eat only when hungry, and stop while still hungry. To test your power of will think of something sickening as you gaze upon your food ; if your stomach rejects the food from that cause, you have no need of any more food at that time—cease eating at once. If you drop your knife, fork, or spoon, or have any such mishap at the table, cease eating. Never think how your food tastes, and never indulge in talk and laughter while eating ; let your thoughts be fixed upon the object to be attained, whether it be the elimination of disease, grossness, bad habits, etc., or the building up of the dual divine nature wherein all power resides.

The one great curse of civilization (?) is gormandizing. We need very little food if the truth were known; just enough should be taken into the stomach to form a nucleus of attraction for the spirit to materialize itself, or condense and form new particles of blood, nerve and flesh. Behold! the miracle of the loaves and fishes as an illustration of this principle. Food multiplies itself in the half-filled stomach, when it is left vacant from a principle; but when the stomach is full there is no room for multiplication or condensation to take place, and a filthy, rotting, destructive process takes the place of divine and life-improving process. The life of the body comes from the spirit, and not wholly from the food we take in at the mouth; of course, the full stomach crowds the spirit out, and there is no room left for the action of the spirit therein. Besides, the spirit feeds upon that which is in harmony with it in its passage to and from, and radiation around, the body, and passing into the body deposits therein that life which it has accumulated. Look at DR. TANNER, fasting forty days! Look at the fast of JESUS for forty days, and then behold GOTTAMA BUDDHA, living seven years alone in the forests of THIBET, subsisting wholly upon berries and roots; and at last throwing himself at the foot of "the sacred Kalpa tree," vowed that he would not again taste food until he had achieved his object, viz., the attainment of supernatural energy; and then when so weak with the long fast that he could no longer stand upon his feet, the "Dewas" (celestial beings) came and fed and nursed him. Did he attain his object? Look at the results and then judge. He lived about five hundred years before Christ, and died when he got ready (at the age of eighty years); founding the greatest religion that man has ever known, whose adherents numbered a few years ago the enormous number of three hundred and sixty-nine millions, and that without violence or bloodshed. (See "Hardy's Eastern Monachism.") Those who eat the least have the best health and last the longest. Life is sustained more from the atmosphere and electricity than from the solid food taken into the stomach. It is the essence of things which is of greatest value, and the essence is not limited to the solid substance, but radiates round about as its aura—intangible to our dull senses, but nevertheless existing. It is upon the aura of things that the spirit feeds, and according to the attractive power of the soul is its pasture. So long as the spirit is fat it will feed the body. The glutton has a weak, lean, hungry spirit, and little will-power. The diseased forms which meet the eye at every turn, are evidence of weak, small, spiritless will—and collapsed and angular souls. They present a ravenous multitude, a standing mockery of nature, and a clamorous rebuke of the wisdom of an infinite Creator. When diseased, in pain and trouble, how nice it is to lay the blame on fate, nature or GOD. But if we would only stop and think that *we have to suffer* from the malignity or mistakes of the relentless power which compels us to exist, and that no prayers are answered save those of the *will*, we would philosophically shoulder the *power* TO BE as much as to

do and to suffer. We could then see clearly that the
diseases, failures and mistakes, ascribed to fate, are due
to our own ignorance, weakness and headstrong folly.
We have to bear the *consequences* of our acts—why not
claim the credit of causation? So long as we can ascribe
our acts to circumstances, nature, fate or GOD, we
trust to luck and drift like bubbles upon the frothing
deep—effortless. It takes effort to accumulate property ;
it takes effort to be a man under all circumstances ;
but it costs no effort to be a beggar or a knave.
This has become so common that it has given rise to
the trite saying, that "man is prone to do evil as
the sparks are to fly upward." It is far easier to fall
than to climb ; but it hurts fearfully at the bottom. The
labor of climbing is pleasant after you get used to it ; for
the higher you climb the more vigorous you become, and
the purer the atmosphere. Why? Because the climber
is ascending towards life, while he who falls is descending
towards pain, disease, weakness, darkness, death, and
nonentity. Will-culture is the royal ladder, anchored in
GOD's throne, and reaching to every soul.

You cannot carry much grossness, either of body,
mind, or spirit, up that ladder. Grossness is always positive, and very difficult to become negative. But the
greater the grossness, the greater the power when the
victory is won. Paul understood this. He says, in substance: "Where sin abounds grace doth much more
abound." I have already explained the reason. It takes a
great soul to excel in anything. Great criminals are always
men of greatness, misdirected. The mind is a wandering

vagrant ; like the eye, it wanders restlessly in quest of new things. But "let your eye be single," and your mind will follow after. Look steadily at a speck on the wall—think steadily of one thing—and gradually there steals over you strange sensations, as clouds and flashes of light pass before your vision. To make the mind single—as an eye with the motes plucked out sees only one object—limit the range of thought. In this you are drawing the mind to a focus preparatory to elongation. As the eye with dust therein sees nothing distinctly, so the mind untrained has no focus, no depth, no clairvoyance ; it wanders in a maze of error.

To call its scattered forces together is a herculean task, but it is small compared to the focusing of the spirit. As involuntary powers follow the lead of the voluntary—as the mind follows the direction of the eye, being fixed when the eye is fixed—so spirit obeys the will. Agitation of the body disturbs the mind ; agitation of the mind distracts and confuses the spirit, so that the will is deprived of its means to execute. Hence the necessity of calmness. Continuity is that which produces rest and satisfaction, as the love of a woman. It is the feminine of will, and *creates* by persistent effort. In deep, profound meditation, the soul becomes pregnant with greatness, for the spirit, no longer driven from the soul by outward motions and emotions, slowly comes home to the soul, being called in and projected upward and inward. As spirit is fire, or that which produces fire, there is heat produced by its accumulation, which in time blazes forth, at first soft and mild, in great sheets of light, afterwards as the forked lightning. This light is life, which feeds the spirit body, and gives it strength and growth. It is in this turning within, this meditation, that the positive will becomes the negative; and when pushed to extremes, total abstraction or forgetfulness follows; this is TRANCE. In trance the angels and celestial spirits are attracted, for the whole universe of spirit impinges upon the soul, by virtue of its attractive power. The Heavens are opened, and there is nothing hid from the truly great will. It pierces to any centre of power, energy, love, or knowledge, and drags therefrom its secrets. This is indeed the closet wherein Jesus told his disciples to enter when they prayed; and to pray in secret, not letting the right hand know what the left hand doeth. In this way is the answer of prayer possible. "God is a spirit, and they who worship Him must worship in spirit and in truth." To be in a trance is to be enveloped in spirit—to be "baptized with the Holy Ghost and with Fire." No deception, no untruth can enter here. Truth elevates the soul, and is a condition requisite to acquisition of all occult knowledge and power. To be true to yourself is to be true to God. To be true to conditions is to be divested of all fear, distrust, and doubt; these bar the way and close the door. An abiding faith in the Infinity of Power, and belief in the ability of the soul to rise to realms thereof, are essentially basic principles of progress. To awaken the soul from its long sleep of the ages, a preparation is necessary. All passions must be put to sleep. The temper must be subjugated, and the animosities of nature must be destroyed. This is a herculean task to most men, but unless this be done, let no one boast of his will-power.

The reason is obvious why these conditions are requisite. The larger the soul the greater the agitation of the elements within its radius; and the passions being the easiest disturbed are all in excessive activity. This explains why many noble-souled men go to the bad. Those capable of soaring the highest fall the lowest when bereft of self-control. The soul is an absolute CALM, and when all things are calm outside it expands itself as if to burst its prison-walls; then the Unnatural rushes upon its prisoner to overcome its power and destroy it. The calm warm sunshine of summer days creates vast vacuums in the atmosphere; then comes the cyclone, the tornado, the lightning. These are nature's passions, which rage till the vacuum is subdued.

The essential office of the soul is to create, and it does this by motions and emotions. Repulsion drives, diffuses, and scatters the spirit abroad. Attraction draws, not only its own to itself, but the aura or spirit of other things, which it appropriates so far as it is able. And this appropriation or fusion of elements is either elevating and life-giving, or is destructive.

The fire of things is life, and there are no compounds thereof—it is one ; but the aura of things is graded from fire to the grossest stench, which united, forms a compound that is not pure. Purity feeds the FIRE-BODY, in which death and destruction have no place. Water in agitation becomes pure ; but stagnant water has *more life* in it than running water. Of course the spirit in con-

centration becomes stagnant for a time, and in this stag·
nation, as in stagnant water, life in myriad forms springs
into being. But ere they have being in the spirit, by
persistent effort of will, in concentration *upon the Idea
of a Divine body*, this life is condensed, or compelled to
take form as ONE. I am aware that there is a spiritual
body which forms at death, but it is not an immortal
body. This has been seen and described by many clairvoyants, and is spoken of by Paul ; but the Divine body
is formed in this body during earth-life, or it is not formed
at all. It is not a compound, neither is it corruptible
matter. It is not seen by you, but you will know of it
by having a feeling of immortal life and undying power
within. When perfected, all power in heaven and in
earth will be yours—not as a man, but as a GOD.

"A mere fancy sketch "—"a picture of a disordered
brain !" Nevertheless, it is a shadow of creative power,
projected from the realm of the incomprehensible beyond ! Is there such a realm? If so, does it contain
things ?

To return to our subject. In the concentration of
spirit is increased life, sensation, sensitiveness, motions,
emotions, and power of all sensuous enjoyments. Hence
many fall into the *slough of sense* on the road, and never
get out.

The body is filled full to overflowing with spirit (magnetism miscalled), and the entire being vibrates with
pleasure-seeking emotions and longings. None but the
pure can pass over this bridge ; the impure fall at "the
threshhold." Monstrous shapes stand guard here—

"Cherubim" with "flaming swords" guarding "the way to the tree of life."

It is the combustion of the compounds in the spirit which causes the commotion, which, if resisted, they become rectified in time.

The road to calmness, tranquility, peace, is first to be thorougly satisfied in your own mind that such is the *only* way to health and happiness. I am not going to argue this point, it is the universal instinct of all thinking, reasonable men—none but savages will dispute it. This point settled, then go to work to attain it. This is done by a constant and eternal watchfulness. As I before stated, the passions must be controlled, subdued, and brought into total and abject subjection to the will. This is best accomplished by setting apart one hour each evening for meditation. During this hour you think only of the weakness and folly of anger, lust, avarice, envy, etc., dwelling most upon your greatest and most besetting weakness in such a manner as to cause you to loathe yourself; think of all you have done during the day—of the thoughts and feelings you have had, especially dwelling upon your failures at self-control; aggravating your follies, and not trying to excuse yourself in the least. If you feel like asking for help, do so, but in thought only, and that the last thing you do, and as briefly as possible.

Compare yourself with the calm, tranquil beauty of a flower, or a twinkling star, and thus take the pride out of your pretended greatness and egotism. Think of the body as needing your utmost care of nursing, as an ulcer

needing to be dressed and poulticed—not that you love
the ulcer, but to assuage its pain.

Only a few years, and loathsome worms will crawl out
and in at its nine orifices, and filthy matter will frost the
lips you now curl so proudly. To destroy any feeling
create its opposite. Is your heart agitated, torn and lacer-
ated with unrequitted love? Does jealousy steal away your
sleep and peace of mind? Kill it then by clothing in your
mind the object in garments of disgust. Rise above it in
your thought, and look down upon it with disgust as an
eagle passes by carrion. Fix your mind upon its worst
and most disgusting aspect; thus forgetting its allurements,
the love grows less and less, until at last you wonder that
you ever had such a feeling. Analyze, dissect the human
heart, turn it over and over, pick it to pieces shred by
shred, and see if you can find its main spring—when
found, it will be just like your own. Do you hate?
Have you an enemy who delights in your woe? Well,
kill your hate, and thus your enemy, by learning to love
him. "Oh! that is impossible," says one. Impossible
only to the weak. The will that cannot create love is a
mere semblance—a bubble; it cannot endure. Christ
said, "Love your enemies." In order to produce love
you must sow the seed first, before it can grow. The
seeds of love are respect. In your meditations fix your
mind upon him and thus evoke his "similacrum," and
compel him to reveal his best nature to you; thus
you can find in all some little good to inspire your
respect. Culture this, losing sight of his deformities and
infirmities of character, for it shall in time ripen into

love to the building up of yourself and him. Are you superior to your enemy? If so, it is only in your love or charity, and not in pretence. "Pray for your enemies." Desire is prayer, which, to be answered, must be so intense that acts go therewith. To pray for your enemy is to do him good—not in the mere breathing of desire, but by kindly looks and acts. A gentle manner, a kind look, or word fitly spoken, an unobtrusive gift always goes to the heart, and will do more to kill enmity and elevate the soul than all the egotism on the globe. Pride, avarice, envy and malice have no wings, they are monsters of the deep, and have their home in the slime; if you harbor them they will carry you down, down. They leave you as you grow calm and tranquil in love-fulness. If you find you cannot grow in love, go down into disgust, and there wallow till the Divine fire is kindled; but do not get disgusted with others—your field of labor is in yourself, in your own passions and weaknesses.

It is out of disgust, as out of the cesspools of hell, that true manhood and spiritual power takes its rise. He who is not disgusted with his own weaknesses and follies remains in them as a hog in his filth.

In man's *natural* state he is *indifferent;* hence, to him there is no good nor evil, no high, no low—all things are alike—indifferent. Like the earth without living things to inhabit it, is simply neither good nor evil. But man in an *unnatural* state is seething, boiling over, raving mad with the fires of lust; he knows nothing of love or its divinity; he scoffs at the idea of the soul-union of the male and the female as the door to immortal life and GODLIKE *energy*.

All habits arise from and have their life in lust. Sexual habits are no exception, and the rules for destroying the taste for food and drink applies to sex-love as well.

The fires of lust flow downward naturally. To reverse this downward tendency is to reverse the entire man. The spirit follows the thought, as the thought is controlled by physical motions or absence thereof. This turning of the operations upward is done only by an increased and extreme action of the brain and nervous system. To charge the brain with blood and increase its magnetic power and action, breathe deeply and constantly through the nostrils—deep, slow, long drawn inspirations, followed by rapid expirations; this, persisted in, becomes in time, a habit, which the soul carries on even in sleep, till the barriers of sense give way, and clairvoyance is the result; but beware of insanity if the mind does not expand first by proper training. The higher mind *ought* to rule, but unfortunately, in most men, body lords it over mind, lust rules the world. The man who by *will* rules and controls his passions is nicely balanced; the man who by will puts his passions to sleep so that they need no watching, has entered already the realm of power; he has withdrawn the sexual fires from the lower extremities to his brain, and only needs to go one step more to become one of the "Illuminati," *i. e.*, *provided he is a passionate man*. ("A passionless man is an infernal monster, not only in this, but in all the starry worlds of space." P. B. RANDOLPH.)

Passion being held and controlled by WILL, and the fires of sex confined to the body, gradually draws together towards the mind; the thoughts collect and run together like a stream of water—shallow and wide at first, spreading away into swamps and marshes—stagnant pools which send up scum and filth, redolent of disease and crime, which, when a channel is dug, collects its waters into a murmuring brook, and gradually becomes a mighty river, purifying its waters by its own motion. The will digs the channel, and gradually draws the thoughts therein. It is hard at first, for they love the freedom of wildwood and slough, where they can bask and sun themselves, and evaporate to nothing; they wash away the tiny banks many times, but the determined WILL builds and rebuilds until the banks are mountains high, and the river a powerful stream, upon which the soul is borne aloft, and angels, descending, meet the lone voyager with comfort and a purer spirit. The heights once ascended, the pathway ever remains, and each succeeding ascent becomes easier and easier. The way once learned, how strong and vigorous—how full of life, peace, rest, and joy, the scene becomes! And yet how lowly innocent and childish! But "the way is a straight and a narrow way." If ye will abide, then dig deep the channel towards the Infinite, and train the fractious thoughts to run therein, until they shall love the way, and all other thoughts be tributary, and run and murmur along the valleys, down the gorges, and leap and dance into the bosom of God.

By concentration alone can man become powerful. Who can select one idea or thing, and think of that alone

to the exclusion of all other thoughts, for the space of
five short minutes? Not many. Yet there are men who
can take one thought, and follow its thread-like form for
hours, as it winds its devious way, increasing as it goes,
until it flows smoothly and noiselessly into the bosom of
the sublime ocean of all truth, wherein they lave to their
soul's content.

Thought comes upon us like the dew upon the earth,
but there are places where there is no dew; but such are
rocks or dry sands; there are no flowers whose opening
petals catch no dew. Some men are like a pool of water,
redolent of filth, whose surface is covered with a yellow-
ish-green scum, which comes not from the atmosphere,
but from within. This scum settles upon the faces of
men, thick here and thin there; and also upon their
lives. It may be seen sometimes with the naked eye; at
other times it flashes out like an adder's tongue, only to
be seen with clairvoyant sight.

This shows that man has only a little time ago come up
out of the water; that some have been out a longer time
than others. There are lizards, snakes, frogs, toads,
birds, spiders, and God only knows what, walking like
men; but genuine men are scarce. They may be known
by their lack of scum. Thought dissipates the scum,
meditation annihilates it. Thought is the lightnings of
God's universe. Men are lightning-rods. Some are so
flat on the top of the head, that they attract nothing
from the clouds that overshadow. Such attract from the
earth; their feet take root; they cannot think, but vege-
tate and gather scum, the filthiest of which is Gold!

Others—and God knows how few they are—by their high, dome-like heads, attract spiritual forces, like the lightnings from the clouds, that shatter and break up the great deeps of their being, searing the outside so that no moss or scum will grow there. Thought burns; it rolls and turns the brain inside out, giving no opportunity for stagnation. Not so the thought that comes from the earth; this stagnates and increases filth.

Purity is oneness. It is the nucleus around which centres all good. It is the magnet of the human soul, and holds our thoughts as one, centred upon the source of all purity, GOD.

By thought, man meditates; and meditation collects the spirit and draws it from outward things to the inner, and leads to abstraction—the forgetting of one's self. Abstraction is the knife that cuts the chords which bind the soul to things. In other words, it finishes what thought begins, and prepares the soul for flight. Magnetic sleep is its weakest phase. In this, the soul goes not out; but the subject often has second sight, and sees to distant places; his power depending upon the combined fires of the operator and himself.

The spirit once concentrated and drawn within, is under the control of the will, and may be projected to any distance, and produce any effect desired, from the impressing of others, and healing the sick, up to moving substances, and the manifesting of phantoms. This is a dual power.

In the culture of will, there are many things demanding attention. The tongue is said to be an unruly mem-

ber ; hence the Rosicrucian adage, " Silence is strength."
In much speaking is evil. Excitement is injurious ; and
the tongue fires and excites passion. The calm man is
the strong man. To control others, first control yourself.
To control spirit, control your passions. To penetrate
the secrets of others, expand your consciousness so as to
come *en rapport* with their inmost being. To feel as
others feel, and thus know them, you must rise *above*
them, then descend *to* them. You are not superior to
anything, only in your *imagination*. Culture this, then,
by looking for pictures in it as in a mirror. To get *en
rapport* with another, you must first see him in your
imagination ; when seen, *command* him, and he will
obey. Clairvoyance is the road to power ; but be so
healthily or not at all. The soul is magical ; it can do
anything ; produce anything, if it be large enough ; then
study to expand it. To project your spirit to any distance, and thus be seen and heard, make the spirit pure
so that it can vie with the lightnings in space, and not
stick like slime to objects on the way. Your soul cannot
travel without a coach, the spirit is the coach. Make
yourself *double*, and then all things are easy. To be
divine, *forget* that you are the devil. Power dwells in
silence, and in secrecy—more in thought than in word—
more in a look than in a blow, if you know how to look.
Many a man has sickened and died, or went crazy, at the
wish of another. Many a man has been haunted to death
by the strong will of another. Many a man has been
made to do the right towards another by that other
forgiving him his wrong long before.

There is more power in forgiveness than in revenge, for the Gods avenge wrongs done to a good man. "Curses come home to roost," but they often do a sight of mischief before they come home, especially when the *outraged soul curses*. If you feel disgust, can you look love? Can you look disgusted when you feel love? If not, "try," for this is will-culture. Can you hold your tongue when another calls you liar, thief, dog? If not, you are no man! *Dogs* snarl and bite at each other. How can you control your spirit, when your tongue is your master? Can you be deaf while another raves? —especially your wife? If not, then you are under the control of others. Get out, man, by all means! Enter into yourself, as in a "closet," and when you have shut your eyes to sight, and your ears to sound, and your nerves to sensation, you have then "shut the door," and "whatever you shall ask the Father in secret shall be done to you openly." This is worshiping "in spirit and in truth."

Water is prolific; all things gestate in water. The waters of the human soul are wrung out of the heart by real or imaginary wrongs. There is no growth without moisture. The dews that give life to vegetation are nature's tears. The great soul has a soft, weeping heart. The small soul has no tears in it to shed.

The true child of "the shadow" has a heart that distils the dews of its sympathy unseen and unknown; it weeps over the fallen, and suffers in secret at its powerlessness to relieve. It is often sad without knowing why. Even adversity in material things does not affect it, as the shadow which seems to brood, like the night, over it. When the shadow comes closest,—when the sun is obscured and the stars give no light,—when hope is wellnigh fled,—look up, child of the gloom! for the light is near by, hidden in the deep folds of the cloud which rests like a pall over you. It is "the brooding" of the spirit —your sense—in your disgust of life and love—which is softening and making malleable your heart of stone. When it is cultured enough, it will produce its fruit—the harvest is sure. Prepare your ground, then—dig deep the ditches for drainage and irrigation ; draw together all your forces in order to pierce the gloom.

The meditations recommended in this work as the true mental and spiritual discipline, are all of a gloomy and sombre character. The reason must be obvious to every thinker. There is a principle underlying this, in perfect harmony with the history of mankind. It is the thoughtless who laugh. It is thought which takes the laughter out of a man and drapes him in black—symbol of the fire. Inspiration comes from despair; and hearts that weep are close upon the confines of a great joy, peace and rest. "Blessed are they that mourn, for they shall be comforted." "God chasteneth whom he loveth," is a hard saying, but it is true. The trouble is, we do not know how to make use of the gloom, or the evil of life. We must learn to *love the shadow*, and to call it to ourselves by a mental effort. "Resist not evil," is apropos here. The great minds who have pierced the gloom, and handed down to mankind light and philosophy, that enables us to bridge the abyss of death, have been sad-hearted, weeping men. "JESUS wept," but we have no knowledge of his ever laughing. GOTTAMA never smiled after he forsook a crown and his family, for the forest and the yellow robes of Asceticism. APPOLONIUS, SOCRATES and PLATO were not laughing men.

There is a chamber of mourning, veiled and draped in black—in every human heart. We all retire to it at times, but the great-souled oftenest. Here the lurid world loses its glare, and all things become sombre; the mind here loses its ferocity, and we go forth subdued. Alas for him who does not ! Alas for him whose experience still leaves him hard within ! whose river of life sends out no waters, no tears, no dew of sadness and sympathy over weaknesses and follies, all too apparent ! Such need much thought—nay ! they need the blows and chastisement of fate—the earthquake, the tremblings of fear, the lightning's rending—the agony of disease, disappointment, hate, jealousy and despair, to compel them to think. But let him, who would steer clear of these, provoke his soul to sadness, by meditations of such a nature as shall make him sick of life and its pleasures. If disease, weakness, pain or sickness bring lucidity of mind, it is well, but if death ensues without it, it is not so well. The mind should grow clearer and stronger from physical suffering, as the soul should expand her wings from mental anguish. To love the evil, and invite it, is to make it good.

At a certain stage of development the soul becomes

self-sustaining and productive of all that is needed. It becomes magical in its physical manifestations, as it is itself; for the soul is a magical thing, and in its expansion—when it has filled the whole man with itself, after having become globular—the body becomes a magical or a divine body.

XVI.—SOUL-POWERS AND SPIRITUAL GIFTS.

There is no limit to man's powers. That which seems a limit disappears or becomes an assistance in the reversal of the thought concerning it. All spiritual gifts come from the lifting of the veil crushed thick and opaque by objective things, or the piercing through of the sight, as a peering under through an opening or rift in the rolling clouds of mundane things. This is about as clear as mud. Let me explain. Mental perception, intuition, or sight of the mind, is in the centre of the intellect; but it ordinarily is a dark sun, which becomes luminous by effort, as I have already set forth. Magnetism is a short road to lucidity, but the powers conferred are weak compared to those which come through effort. Magnetization is effected through passivity, and the vacating of thought and will. But it alternates, *i. e.*, depends upon conditions which vary, and are sometimes favorable and sometimes unfavorable; and consequently, it is subject to spells—comes and goes, and leads everywhere and anywhere. It is good enough so far as it goes, but it does not go deep enough or far enough. The magnetic sleep is not at all dependent upon purity nor will-power. The luminosity I teach is not a sleep necessarily; it is a blindness, or a cutting off of externals—a separation of the selfhood from outward influences by the sinking in or absorbtion of the voluntary powers, or the growth of the involun-

tary to the voluntary, so that they beco   one. Mes--
meric sleep is the first phase of it.   Illumination, when
once reached through and by effort of will, is always
available.   It makes and preserves uniform conditions;
hence it has no "fits or starts," and makes no failures.
When perfect it cannot be lost, for it is death-proof, and
its possessor is no *subject* of any power in existence.   He
is an immortal being, having divine powers.   There are
many grades of powers, but I will first speak of sight:
first, natural sight; second, clairvoyance; third, soul-sight.
    Clairvoyance has several degrees, while natural sight
has only one.   The first degree of clairvoyance is similar
to natural sight: *i. e.*, it sees only objects, such as reading blindfolded; seeing objects at a distance; seeing
through matter, etc.   It grows by practice, and its powers increase as the lucidity of the brain increases.   But
lucidity is simply dependent upon the purity of the
spirit.   Purity focalizes the spirit, but magnetization is a
result of a mixture of spirits; hence it is what I have
defined as impurity or an adulteration.   It is exalting, as
an intoxication; hence its effects are fleeting and ephemeral in proportion to the impurities involved.   I do not
mean by impurities, immoralities at all.   Impurity is in
the mixture and appropriation of different auras, substances, magnetisms, etc.   Magnetic subjects go into the
condition and come out of it through the influence of an
operator; sometimes in the form, but often out of it.
In either case they are subject to the will of another, and
the lucidity or exaltation of powers is a result of the
union of spirits both in the form and out, which disap-

pears when the subject is out of the condition. But the effects do not disappear so readily. Often the subjects are a prey to vampires both in the form and out, under whose infernal " sucking " the life is slowly but surely sapped. This is the case with more people—especially women—than many imagine. There is a conscious and an unconscious vampirism. All mediums are not, however, subject to this curse. Space will not allow me to dwell upon this important subject, farther than to add that mediumship is not confined to the ranks of Spiritualism. Nine-tenths of all the crimes committed are due to vampirism. A vampire is not necessarily a *disembodied* spirit; we are just as much spirits now as we will ever be, and all the power that any spirit may have we can have, if we only know how to develop and use it. For that which is not in us cannot exist long as ours. Clairvoyance is a mental power, and as the mind becomes more and more luminous by practice and focalization of the spirit, "spiritual gifts" are joined to it, as fruit is joined to a blossom. It is not my object to specify and define these gifts further than is necessary to elucidate my subject.

Vampirism is one spirit preying upon another. It differs from obsession in degree only. Clairvoyance becomes deeper and deeper by practice, until it enters somewhat into the penetralia of things, in which its subject becomes alive to influences—aches, pains, physical and mental states, aspirations, loves, longings, etc. It is now becoming near to another power, viz: the perception of spirit forms, faces, and the hearing of voices, or clairaudience. This is, of course, a higher power than mere sight of objects. Spirit pours out in look and gesture, but in speech more than in any other manner. In fact, speech is the highest expression of spirit, and it is more susceptible to culture than looks or gestures, and leads to greater depths of being ; and is moreover more reliable, because it does not lead to that idolatry which the sight of beauty and grandeur always does. The beholding of spiritual beings by clairvoyants has led many into the erroneous idea that they have beheld GOD, the ineffable ONE, when, in fact, such sight may be a conjuration of the will of some strong operator. Phantoms seldom speak ; to be reliable, sight and hearing should go together.

The deepest clairvoyance is that where objects, both material and spiritual, are passed by as of no account ; and the ineffable glories of soul-realm glimpsed. This is a sight of spirit, as fire only, and not as objects. This fire or spirit finds a voice suited to the ear of him who will listen.

ZOROASTER said : "When you see the fire, listen to the voice of the fire !" It was in view of this truth that MOSES enacted laws against the communicating with spirits ; and in order to preserve purity in the mediums (or priests), tried to confine it to the tribe of LEVI. It was for this purpose (purity) that celibacy was enjoined by BUDDHA. Beyond this mundane sphere—beyond the realm of spiritual things — is infinite knowledge and power. And he who is able to pierce through the shadow which things casts, sees the glories of the spirit-worlds.

But this is all. Forms do not appear from beyond "the abode of the GODS;" but he who can visit the highest abode may hear the echoes of busy feet, and the whisperings of incomprehensible and unutterable things. This power I call SOUL SIGHT; but it is not a sight of things, but of the fire of principles. This power is *within* all spiritual powers. As the soul is the inmost of the man, so is soul-sight the inmost of intuition. Clairvoyance, psychometry, and clairaudience, are all developed by contact, or the coming *en rapport* with objects. Their field of operations is in the spirit of things; but soul-sight is developed by holding the spirit aloof from other things, spirits, etc. And the losing sight of all distinctions or differences of things. It is the *distinctness* of things which scatters the spirit and confuses thought and mind. We know nothing, because there are *so many things to learn*. He who seeks the *absolute* loses sight of the differences of things, and passing inward, reaches the spirit thereof; but instead of entering *en rapport* therewith, passes deeper still, *beyond all distinctions* and differences to the oneness of being—in fact, to the SUPERNATURAL of his own being. "He that hath a mind to think, let him think;" for, indeed, it is thought which leads to hearing of the Word. This is the real meaning of JOHN: "In the beginning was the Word, and the Word was with GOD, and the Word was GOD." He who passes in thought through and beyond things, hears "the Word of GOD." For GOD dwells in the inmost recesses of all being, hidden away from all mortal sight; hence the necessity of destroying the differences of things

in the mind. The differences among men constitute
hell. How easily we are all brothers when we forget our
differences. They make enemies of us—enemies to each
other and to GOD. How harmonious we would be if
there were no distinctions. Of a truth, this is the road
to GOD. The man who fixes not his attention upon differences of race, sex, conditions, opinions, names, etc.,
is a great-souled man, and looks with indifference upon
the small things which agitate and disturb mankind. He
can lay claim to kinship with GOD, who loves all alike.
Aye, and he holds sweet converse with GOD in the depths
of his own all-knowing INTUITIVE SOUL !

This is the source of all inspiration. GOD finds voice
in the soul, and intuition is but the faint echoes thereof,
as it vibrates along the dark and noisome crypts of being.
Alas ! for him, who " hath no ears to hear ; " nor " eyes
to see "—his darkness must be intense indeed. Let him
who would reach the regal powers of the soul sit in circles.
For in the mingling of magnetisms is an intense and
fierce combustion or war of spirits produced, in which
conflagration, great and rapid changes take place ; during
which the soul begins to make motions as of a thing
coming to life ; it is drawing itself together into shape,
leaving the atoms of the body. Motions are usually felt
first in the hands, which vibrate somewhat like when in
contact with a magnetic battery ; this sensation extends
in time to every part of the body in some persons ; in
others, it is limited to the hands, arms or head ; it deepens
in intensity till the nerves begin to twitch and jerk. Now,
when you have got thus far, there are two roads open for

you. If you wish mediumship with any of its multitudinous phases, with a band of helpers and a guide, *just sit passive* and "let it jerk;" don't expect or be anxious for anything, but let yourself alone, fully resigned to accept whatever may come without doubt or criticism. Think of nothing as nearly as possible, and above all *resist no impulse of thought, word or action.* "Follow your impulses" is *the* law of mediumship. But if you choose the SOUL ROAD, you must now brace yourself for an effort; that effort is RESISTANCE—resist all impulses and all motions of the nerves and muscles; instead of passivity, grasp yourself as with your hands, holding fast in your mind or imagination with the same tension of the nerves as if you were holding something, but *without any muscular contraction*—this while sitting in the circle.

To become spiritual, cultivate mind, for this is the door which must, indeed, open before you can walk out into the realms of power. To cultivate mind, increase the activity of the nervous system and its source—the brain. Draw the blood to the brain, by deep breathing and the fixing of the thought upon the object in view. Magnetize yourself one hour every evening by taking hold of the left thumb with the right thumb and forefinger, and pressing gently, enough to keep the attention fixed upon it, and think of one thing, say some word—your own name, if nothing else—saying it over and over to yourself constantly. In a short time your object will become fixed and constant in your thoughts, and the soul will begin its work. But remember that each effort you make upward will be followed by a revulsion downward, and you will find yourself becoming amorous. Resist this impulse, as all impulses : in the course of time, you will see clouds, flashes of light, and faces or forms will peer out of the gloom at you, or form in the clouds. Pay *no attention* to these things, but keep right on with your exercise. There are many more methods which I am not at liberty to disclose. Things of a *physical* nature assist the physical, inasmuch as physical nature yields most readily to such things as are like itself, or one degree removed therefrom. To illustrate : a brute yields to the force of a club, but when he is trained a word controls him. So with mankind : some need kings, and soldiers with bayonets, to keep them within humanity's realm ; others stay there naturally, for they understand its unspoken and unwritten laws. For babes, milk and baby-talk ; for children, play-houses and stories ; for youth, the dance and the opera ; for middle age, the rush and rattle, the clash and commotion of business ; for mature man, thought, reason, spiritual things. These are nature's methods of culture. *Nature cannot be forced out of one mood into another.* Ask yourself, "Where does my love lead me?" and nature or your own soul will tell you truly. If you long to become spiritual, begin at once, and that gradually. " Nature allows none to overleap her barriers ; they must be *beaten down.*" Don't ask GOD to teach you, but learn of such as are in harmony with you, even if it be the devil.

The basis of all understanding is mutual sympathy existing between the teacher and the taught—the actor and the acted upon. To the material in thought, desire and action, are the matter-of-fact in nature adapted. They are like it, and hence the spiritual is too far removed from them to be their direct teachers; such need physical training, and to them are physical means necessary. Hence, to such (and in fact, all men are of this class more or less), in addition to deep breathing, the bath, in cold, magnetic water; a complete and radical change in the diet; rest instead of exercise; thought instead of talk; tears instead of laughter; darkness instead of light; emotion instead of motion—these and more are necessary to train the physical *before the spiritual can come forth.* Spirit is formless, and yet not altogether so. There is a form within these bodies of ours, which is spirit, and yet it hath no form until detached, as it were, from the flesh. All development is a loosening of the spirit from the flesh and the loves thereof; and this loosening is the embryotic organization of the spiritual body carried on and fully perfected.

Resist muscular and nervous motion with all your power of will. KEEP CALM. Never allow any circumstance to agitate or disturb you; for here in the degree of motion it is that demons and evil-disposed spirits take advantage of your sensitive and expansive condition, and enter in—first, the nervous system, and secondly, the mind, and control you to your destruction. Music sets you on fire, and you want to dance, sing or shout: keep silent—"silence is strength!" Never debate! But let the one object be to keep calm, self-possessed and cool. This is the beginning of self-control and power. It is *concentration.* Think, meditate, read and study—but keep silent. Remember there are beings around you who come in connection with you through words, sounds, motions, etc., who, without them, remain ignorant of your object and condition. There are demons and spirits who cannot read the mind, but who can hear and see.

It is when thrown off our guard, being carried away by strange sensations, thoughts, impulses, motions and emotions, that we are seized upon by the *above* or *below*, and carried away from ourselves, as it were, from our equipoise or balance—self-consciousness dethroned : and we rise or fall according to predisposition. The falling into acts silly and criminal, or *less* than those of the normal state, is termed "OBSESSION ;" but this, like most names, is an effort to *explain* that which we do not understand ; an assumption of knowledge ; an excuse we make to ourselves for our ignorance ; a *distinction* made ; a difference, visible in extremes, as good and evil, which flow into one another as one ; but to us, and for us, obsession is as real as the evil, and must be avoided.

Since I commenced writing this book, this subject was forced upon my attention by a series of articles in some one of the spiritual papers ; I cared nothing for the differences of opinion in regard to obsession ; but feeling the necessity of progress in the avoidance of evil, by *some persons* at least, I sought for a sure, safe and certain preventive of it ; I pondered several days upon this subject with no satisfactory result. One night, alone in my tent, a wave of loneliness and sadness swept over me. This had no visible or mundane cause—my health was excellent, business was good, money was plenty (for I had "a dime in my pocket," which is enough as long as it lasts), but nevertheless I was low-spirited ; I could neither think nor write, so throwing down my pen I paced up and down until wearied ; I threw myself upon my bed to sleep ; my mind became tranquil as my body became at rest, and this idea of obsession came over me as a problem unsolved. To solve it, I knew of only two ways : One was to come *en rapport with the spirit of obsession*, and hence become *obsessed myself* in order to know by experience all about it, so as to show how to avoid it ; the other was by inspiration.

The first was repugnant to all my thoughts and feelings. Under all circumstances I wish to be myself— and only that ; so I turned aside and repelled the spirit by the thoughts of my own individual selfhood, and the determination to be only myself. There are lights, clouds, flashes, faces and forms here at this condition of the mind ; but I, in following my thought, passed them by as of no account. Laughing faces, hideous faces, and monstrous forms looked out of the light at me, and as I passed by, mocked and scowled. Gradually the lights paled, the faces grew dim and finally disappeared, leaving me in intense and opaque darkness. Pulsating, throbbing, vibrating with strange and weird sensations, I glided along down the corridors of the soul as one falling, and slowly, oh ! so slowly, losing myself. All at once, from out the darkness, and close to me, a voice low and soft sounded in my ear : " To avoid obsession, keep the body positive and the mind negative." The voice came so suddenly, and was so close to me that I was startled and driven back to myself. There I lay all vibrating with ecstatic emotions, altogether out of the ordinary nature of things, with the words engraved in letters of fire upon my consciousness. To me this was a new idea; it was a revelation of a wonderful truth, and I cast about for the logic of it, which is this:

Ordinarily the body is negative, and hence receptive to impressions—physical, atmospherical, and spiritual. The first effect of magnetism is to increase this negative state of the body; hence, it becomes very impressible and very liable to take on the conditions of others, both in the mundane and the spiritual. The will is the cause of all positiveness of mind, body, and spirit. By its force it is repulsive, and holds at a distance things foreign and injurious. Now, in passivity, the will relaxes the tension of the nerves, and they are unstrung; in which state, spirits both good and evil can enter into the inactive sphere of the spirit, and thus get a lodgment from which to control, in time, the mind, and subjugate the will. Now, if by any process the body can be kept positive, the spirit is rendered so, also; and hence, no spirits but those of a negative character will be attracted. Now, it is *only positive* spirits that seize upon and obsess mortals. They are the *repulsive* and the deficient—the empty of sympathy and all elements of greatness. The law is for the positive to enter into and control the negative, *i. e.*, to beget therein their own devilishness. Now, in rendering the mind negative by constantly keeping down its excitabilities, it is elevated by the motive or object in view; and as mind can only be acted upon by mind, and is not a receptacle of anything but ideas, minds of a high order, such as have ideas to give, are attracted, and instil their ideas or thoughts of a positive nature into the negative mind; thus leading the mind upward without disturbing the will in the least. Indeed, such spirits increase the individuality by assisting instead of controlling. Negative spirits never do harm. It only remains for me to explain how the body can be rendered positive, and the mind negative. The tranquil, peaceful, inoffensive mind is negative. This idea of controlling mind instead of nerves and muscles, engages the entire attention and will; for the mind is not rendered tranquil save by constant watchfulness, and the keeping down of those passions which disturb, agitate, and thus cause filth to rise up as impurities of the blood and spirit. The will thus engaged in rendering the mind negative or tranquil, renders the body positive at the same time, because two negatives cannot exist together, neither can two positives. I am aware it is a reversal of nature's methods, but he who would rise up to power must rise in the mind, or not at all. God dwells in all things alike, but those who seek him cannot find him so readily in some things or conditions as in others. Remember what I have previously said about diet. Don't be in a hurry, for all things grow slowly. Weakness is only an argument in favor of strength, and the small measure of the spirit meted out to us here only indicates the vastness of its extent and power. The impossibilities of our infirmities indicate the possibilities of those who are firm. Then doubt not, waver not, but keep steadily, coolly on, up the mountains of difficulty, each one you surmount only reveals more clearly to you the possibilities of your nature. The value of things is in their use. Spiritual gifts are of use just now, in the "a-b-c" of man's growth—in the awakening of man's dull senses to the recognition of a future existence and its nature; but when such becomes universal, as it must in time, what will be their use?

The world has been as far advanced in spiritual things in the long ago as now—and probably much further; but what use was it to them? They had their oracles and their temples, and GODS and *guides* without number; but all this did not prevent retrogression. The ground must now all be traveled over again. Again must the priesthood be organized, the temples built, the altars reared, and the fires lighted; and what is all this for? Oh, the patience of the Infinite! In vain are the choicest gifts of heaven showered upon unthankful and unthinking man! They are all prostituted to devilish ends and aims. The choicest oracles of the olden time led opposing armies to the slaughter of each other. The prophets of the Lord anointed KINGS and watched over the welfare of one nation to the detriment of another. Gifts were all prostituted to the attainment of material wealth, grandeur, glory, and fame. All powers were bent and warped to the creation and perpetuation of monstrous distinctions among men, by reason of which war and outrage are the rule, and peace and harmony *very rare exceptions.* Where now are they? A slow, lingering decay—an awful disease of the very vitals, or

the violent conflagration of their own passions hath
swept them away. The wand of a magician hath waved
across the sky and they are not! But they have left
the diseases which they created behind them in the
ruins of their former glory and worship. Their spir-
ituality is only a ruin. In vain do men teach and
preach; the world goes on in the old beaten track,
and religion follows the lead. In vain did the lowly
JESUS heal the sick and teach the ignorant. In vain
did he cry from the mountains and temples of a rare
good life *here*, free from disease and death. The Jews
heard him not—and now—even *now!* with all our
boasted progress and civilization the word of a GOD is
prostituted to mean something he never intended. "If
ye believe ye shall not die," is enunciated in words
which can have no other meaning. If he had meant
what is now preached as the gospel, it was as easy to have
said "He that believeth shall not go to hell" as to have
said what he did. His teachings from beginning to end
show his mission to have been to teach mankind how to
live humane lives so as to be healthy and happy. His
healing of the sick shows that the gospel was that of physical health and the salvation from disease. His raising of
the dead, and his own resurrection, show further that
death was a thing to be overcome by living a true life.
"And these signs shall follow those that believe," etc.
(See Luke xvi., 17, 18). In another place he says,
"Greater works than these shall ye do, because I go
to the Father." Of what avail are spiritual gifts if
their utmost power is simply to demonstrate another

life without joining this life thereto as one. It must be evident to every thoughtful person that the object of these manifestations is the elevation of the race. And wherein can this be effected, save in the power to enjoy? Where does this power reside, save in health? In vain did Jesus heal the sick if he did not teach the way to *continued* health! In vain did he raise the dead if he did not show the way to *remain* alive! If they die not in the spirit-world, what need of death here? All the revelations heretofore given have been of an immortal life in some other state of existence. *But I tell you of an immortality of this life.* I believe JESUS taught the way of its attainment, but it was not understood. I may not be able to point the whole road, but what I have said already must contain the principles of it in part. Man creates himself and all the essentials of his being—his health, happiness, heavens and hells. But hell comes from misdirected effort; and heaven from *well directed* effort. Things superior descend as a revelation in answer to a demand, which revelation is an *idea—this is enlightenment.* No matter how, or in what manner an idea comes, if it is of a superior character, it is of the light. Hence it is enlightening, and leads upwards. Man must first have an idea of what he wants before he can create conditions *superior* to things that now are.

The *demand always precedes* the supply. Is there a demand for a continuous and happy life here on this globe? Is there a demand for power to create forms of matter for use by effort of will, without the toil and demoniac scramble after the necessaries of life? There will be a demand when man is satisfied of its possibility. Then multiply the mediums! The spirit-world is drawing near. Soon, spiritual beings will walk among us as men—will heal the sick, cast out devils, multiply bread for the hungry, and gold for the greedy, till it shall lose its value, and man turns his attention to the attainment of spiritual powers and gifts. The demand for self-government and peace has already gone up to the GODS, and the answer is coming. The bomb which carried ALEXANDER of Russia into hell, or out of it, was God-sent, in answer to the prayer of many an earnest soul. A full and complete answer is at hand, when the world shall be *free*, and every man shall be his own king, priest, bishop, pope, and GOD! All hail to the mediums and to spiritual gifts of all grades and kinds! For here is freedom. Let gifts be no longer prostituted by individual ambition, nor to the building of THRONES or national GLORY! Let the universal anthem be, " PEACE ON EARTH, GOOD-WILL TO MEN !

Let us work mentally and spiritually, so that the new temple shall not be made with hands of material substance, but a temple in these bodies—a divine body, wherein God shall be conscious to each one of us. Let us rear altars in our own hearts—altars of love-worship, needing no typical sacrifices of the blood of animals or of men. Let us light the fires of the spirit thereon, which are unquenchable and eternal.

Man's desires for immortality have been misdirected, inasmuch as his revelations have been of a *future* life, and not of this. The time has come when revelations must be made of this life and its possibilities—of the present, and not of the future. The perfect life of to-day admits no doubt nor fear of to-morrow. A perfect life here is as fully and completely immortal as any life in any world. The idea of living for the future is a false light; it is a material light of "Lucifer, Son of the morning." Happiness is not of to-morrow, nor of any future time or world. It is to-day or not at all. All life is of to-day and the present. The future never comes. Salvation is from disease. If you die of disease, you wake up on the other side diseased; you have to be cured there before you have fulness of life. The same knowledge that saves you there will save you here. Then why not have that knowledge? The self-same power that feeds the angels in heaven will feed you here, if it is yours. Then why not open your soul to its reception? Heaven is in no particular *place*. It is within you if you want it there, with all its angels and powers—aye! and its immortal life, also. "In union there is strength." "Again, I say unto you that if two of you shall agree on earth as touching anything that they shall ask, it shall be done for them of my Father which is in Heaven." (Matthew xviii., 9.)

This agreement spoken of here is not merely of the mind—it is a union or oneness of spirit, wherein power is multiplied in an unknown ratio. The spirit of one is not as another—they differ in quality, hence there is no agreement: even where minds agree, the spirits do not. Hence the possibility of the truth of the above is in the agreement. Agreement is the kingdom of power. The union of two is of higher quality than one alone; and the more spirits there are in the union the greater is the power. But the difficulty deepens when it is made known that *two male spirits* CANNOT *agree*. Agreement is of the male and female. Herein Divinity appears, and power to accomplish all things is manifest. But union of spirit is preceded by mental agreement. Now, the demand for immortal power and life on this earth must first be a mental agreement, which, in its perfection and harmony, will give birth to union or agreement of *spirit* touching that thing. But look you! WOMAN IS NOT FREE ! Alas for the dawn of light! Woman a slave ! Prostituted by man's selfishness and lust ! How can the prayers of such a monster be answered? "Verily I say unto you," " the prayers of the wicked availeth nothing."

Little can be effected without freedom. But let us do what we can in the union of minds. Spirit works by methods beyond the mind ; hence its laws cannot be comprehended by the mind. " The kingdom of heaven cometh not by observation," *i. e.*, not through laws of mentality. Spirits are unable to explain it. I believe material is evolved from the medium, and combined with subtle elements in the atmosphere by the effort of the will of some powerful spirit, or by the union of several, into flowers, apparitions, spirit-forms, clothing, etc., etc., and that it will yet be demonstrated that materialized spirits *are evolved from the medium*. But no matter how it is done, the power that can make a flower, or a piece of cloth, can make gold, fruit, bread, or anything else desired. All that is requisite are conditions, and knowledge, or faith, or will, or whatever you feel like calling the power. These manifestations are in their infancy as yet,

for, although as old as man, they have probably never been
properly understood, or so universally understood by
spirits of a high and intelligent order as now. They are
experimenting, and they understand fully the value of
co-operation or harmony. The much-talked-of *conditions*
of spiritual manifestations are nothing more nor less.
JESUS, in view of this principle, selected twelve Apostles
who were as harmonious with him as men can well be.
But the Scriptures are mostly silent in reference to the
important part the women who followed him took in the
work he did. It is doubtful if he ever explained this idea
to them; probably this is the esoteric part of the Gospel
which was never written. It is reasonable to infer as
much, for the early Christians had everything in common, thus striving to destroy *distinctions* and to perfect
a union that should enable them to carry out the intuitions and work of JESUS. (See ACTS iv., 32.) "And
the multitude of them that believed were of *one heart*
and *one soul:* neither said any of them that aught of
the things which he possessed was his own; but they
had *all things common"*: that is, the writer *thought* they
were of "one heart and soul" because they *tried* to
be so. Why they gradually lost the gifts of the Spirit
must be evident to every reasonable, thoughtful mind.
The agreement or union was lost through the gradual
growth of *distinctions* and differences:—first, of mind; second, of spirit; and third, of material substances (property).
Had they *perfected the union,* instead of proselyting, they
would have established the church upon a "rock," and
afterwards the growth would have been a steady, healthy,

upward growth; neither would they have wanted for anything, for the kingdom of harmony contains all things.
"First seek the kingdom of heaven: then all other
things shall be added unto you."

This idea of union is corroborated in our own time,
in many ways, notably so in the work of DR. HOTCHKISS,
of St. Louis, Mo., known as "THE DIRTY DOCTOR,"
"THE SNAPPING DOCTOR," and, as he terms himself,
"KING OF MAGNETISM." He has performed as many, if
not more, miraculous cures of diseases than any *healer* of
our day. In 1871 he had six apostles, termed by him
"Radiators," who sat in a row, at times silent and dumb,
behind the class of sick which Hotchkiss treated by
simply snapping his fingers. At other times, "as the
spirit moved them," they joined in the snapping, or
rolled and wallowed in the dirt of his floor, which was
never swept. They lived apart from the world as much
as possible, and were celibates; but HOTCHKISS had a
wife and several other women shut up from contact with
other people—as nuns are kept in a convent. To show
how particular he was in regard to his women I will
relate the following: Wishing to see Dr. Hotchkiss, and
not finding him at his office, I called at his house; a
woman opened the door and asked what I wished. I
explained, not finding the Doctor at home, I wished
to leave a letter for him, which I offered to her. She
drew back as if it were poison, and closing the door in
my face, told me to shove the letter under his office
door. We know very little of the subtle influence of
spirit, or of the effect that the inoculation of one spirit

into another produces. The shaking of hands and kissing
are *sometimes* injurious. Emma Hardinge visited the
Doctor, and has testified to his wonderful magnetic power.
He still lives in St. Louis, a very old man, but as lithe
and supple as a boy; a man of good education and of fine
intellectual powers ; courteous and affable at times, but
sometimes very rude. His " Radiators " left him in
1871 or 1872, I think, and he afterwards had smallpox ;
his wife has gone insane, I have been told ; still he heals
the sick, claiming that he cannot die till Christ comes.
He is not a spiritualist, and is as bitter towards spiritualism as *any* bigot can be. His age is unknown, but undoubtedly it is very great—so great that he has been
termed " *the wandering Jew.*" He is the dirtiest man I
ever saw. I might write a not very small book upon
his eccentricities, customs, antics and cures ; but he never
explains the philosophy of them to anyone; or if he explains anything to-day, he explains it differently another
day. I am satisfied that the secret of his power is fast locked
in the walls where the women are kept. The power that
comes of perfect union or harmony is wonderful. GOD
dwells in it ! "Where two or three are gathered together
in my name"—or in oneness of heart, mind, soul and
spirit—" there am I in the midst." The principle is
what we need—the name or the man is nothing ; but for
those incapable of comprehending a principle, the name
is of vital importance. Do not destroy a man's idols, *if*
he is incapable of reason. The spirit, by union, ascends
higher than if alone ; and GOD descends upon its tide to
bless not merely those who unite, but all the world in

which they move. Alas! for the angularities and differences that destroy us. The secret of union is in *self-harmony* as a foundation : this is good, but *two* is better ; *but if the two be male and female, it is* BEST. Magnetism leads thereto. It behooves me to add, in this connection, that the age of wrong and bloodshed is nearly past. The dawn of a divine government is at hand, wherein the fundamental principle of government is for the *moral benefit* of the *person punished*, and not primarily for the *protection of society*. As a tender and kind father corrects his child for the child's good, and not to vindicate his power or authority in the least, so will society deal with its weak members. Crime will be treated as a disease of the mind, and hospitals will take the place of jails, penitentiaries and scaffolds. Instead of physicians, chaplains and guards, there shall be a few chosen ones who, united in mind and soul, shall pour the *psychological power* of the *angel-world* upon criminals of all classes, and they shall be healed ; for under this influence certain organs of the brain may be rendered inoperative, and other organs may be called into activity ; thus the morally weak may be strengthened, and the depraved shall be made to loathe and despise their depravity ; this can be done in secret without the criminal's knowledge. Who shall lead off in this great moral work. Psychometry will reveal the peculiarities of children and adults, and those needing treatment will be treated and trained without the rod and the dunce-cap. There will be no escape for their criminals, for the mediums will point them out—for *his good* primarily, and secondly, for the good of society. The weak will be known *before* a manifestation of weakness—or, rather, the commission of crime. The time will come, and that speedily, when from the Temples of the ROSE CROSS such power shall be breathed out upon the people, so gently, and so peacefully, that none shall be disposed to do any one a wrong.

The whole people shall join in one grand PSYCHO-LOGICAL effort to banish *disease* and *death* from the land. Who shall say it will not be done? Who will be the first to enroll their names among the Temple-builders and pioneers of the millenium?

Who is there, of all who read this book, that are willing to "TRY?" This is the magic watchword, *Try!* The principles conveyed in the foregoing pages are sufficient to form a basis of union, and he or she who feels in harmony therewith, and is willing to "Try," will find "The Door" to such union indicated in the dedication of this work. To all such I say: "Knock and it shall be opened unto you! Seek and ye shall find!"

XVII.—" ROSICRUCIÆ."

Reference has been made in the preceding pages to the Rosicrucians ; and the work in the main is claimed to be an embodiment of their principles : not all bodied forth, however, by any one sect, class, clime or era ; and it is well, in closing, to anticipate the query as to who, what and where are the ROSICRUCIANS ? That will naturally arise in the minds of most people, because there is so little known of them. And it is well also as corroborative proof and practical illustration of the principles set forth, to cite a few out of many instances in modern times, wherein the possibilities of our nature is made manifest ; for I hold that GOD is no specialist, and what one can do another can do in a greater or less degree under the same *training* and *circumstances*. At least our motto is, "TRY ! "

The Rosicrucians may more properly be termed a fraternity than an order ; albeit many attempts have been made in modern times to *materialize* it as an order, some of which are a success, though of necessity veiled in profound secrecy. The Rosicrucians are numerous— of all nationalities and all climes ; but they are scattered. They meet occasionally—not drawn together by " press notices " or the ringing of bells, but by the moving and drawing of the spirit—as " of one accord."

They were known in history among the other appellations

as the ESSENES, the ILLUMINATI, etc., but since CHRISTIAN ROSENCRUTZ's time, as the Rosicrucians. It was evidently once the universal religion—long ere written history began ; for evidences of " FIRE-worship " are scattered over all the earth in the form of Rosicrucian symbols. The curious reader is referred to HARGRAVE JENNINGS' great work, entitled " THE ROSICRUCIANS," published in England. There was a time when all learned men believed in magic, (another term for magnetism), and those who studied the occult forces of nature, and practiced the powers derived therefrom, were styled priests, and later, magicians ; but after. the destruction of the Magi of Persia, and during the rise of Catholicism, magic became associated with the idea of diabolism, and was styled " Black Art," and all who practiced it were shunned, and sometimes hunted to death. Wherever GOD is found among men you will find a spirit of investigation into the mysteries of being, and a corresponding love of freedom: hence, the true man is free to dig deep or take intellectual flights—aye, even to GOD's throne, and there question him face to face. There is nothing too sacred or secret for him to question for the truth. Recognizing the possibility of the great good, GOD, and the *impossibility* of the DEVIL, they laughed in secret, (for they dared not even *smile* publicly), at priests, bishops, cardinals and popes, and treasured the ancient lore in cypher, and worshipped the undying, unquenchable fire, while they dwelt in caves, or fled before the terrors of the inquisition. This revived the ancient Pagan secret societies and mysteries. To learn and know something more than ordinary is dangerous when such knowledge is unpopular, or, at least, when the masses are ruled by ignorance and superstition. It was at the cost of life to be known as a member of such secret orders—hence arose the proverbial secrecy of the brethren of the ROSY CROSS. Time was when no man would admit that he belonged to that mystic fraternity; furthermore, they shrouded themselves in a cloud of mysteries—not, perhaps, with a view of mystifying others so much as from the idea that all power is a mystery, and that "GOD'S ways are mysterious and past finding out," and they wish to be ·God-like. Rosicrucia is intensely and transcendentally spiritual—hence, it has nothing in common with materialism, except intellectually, and even then the conclusions of materialism are all reversed. It has no affinity with this mammon-worshipping age—hence, it has no golden basis or "insurance plan " to lure men into a *semblance* of brotherly love and fellowship. Unobtrusive, unpretending men, they pass mainly unnoticed through life; they look with pity upon a world of gold- and treasure-gatherers as upon children heaping dirt in the streets. No wonder such men are not understood; they are in the world, but they feel they are not of it, and they wish to get done with it as quietly as possible. Knowing they can leave it only by doing good, they are always secretly doing all within their power. Indeed, they are conscious of having been sent here for that purpose—to help the world in its efforts to humanize the race. The Alchemists of the middle ages believed in the " ELIXIR OF LIFE and the PHILOSOPHER'S

STONE," and diligently sought for them. To drink of the former was eternal youth and life; the latter was sought as a universal solvent, in the use of which the baser metals were changed or transmitted into pure, virgin gold. No wonder these men were called insane; but, nevertheless, they gave the world the principles of chemistry and medicine. Think you such men were fools? Nay! but they had an *idea* which the masses could not comprehend, and they masked it in material that they could grasp. No philosopher ever supposed for a moment that matter in any form could confer immortality upon any other form whatever, for there is no changeless substance in existence. That there is a power in the human soul capable of eternally renewing youth and beauty is a cardinal doctrine of the ROSY CROSS. As to the transmutation of metals, it is not only possible, but true. The idea is of kin to the first; they constitute "the Secret" of the order; but to the true Rosicrucian the latter is of no value whatever, further than as used in the middle ages as an excuse to stop too close espionage, and to compel the *respect*, not only of common people, but the patronage and protection of those in authority, for the practice of alchemy, or dealing even with his "Satanic Majesty" for the purpose of enriching the earth with gold, would be deemed a laudable avocation. They, at least, found protection in it, although prizing it not—for the true adept has all he needs of all things without resorting to any such resource, for he needs but little. There is a providence for every man and woman who stands high enough in the scale of being to be conscious of it, and to be its recipients. The ravens fed the prophet Elijah in the olden time.

Not every man can be an adept in anything, for this capability is born in a man as genius is. Neither is it possible for every man to be a Rosicrucian, no more than education can impart sense; or no more than a child born blind could be made a master artist by learning the terms used to designate the philosophy of light and shade and blending of colors. There must be an innate feeling of rapture at the bare idea of mystery; a hunger and thirst for the unknown, and a conscious and abiding belief in one's own immortality. Such are initiated with profit to themselves and mankind; for in Rosicrucia's Temple they eat and are filled, and drink to thirst no more. Here they find teachers and brothers. We are the children of "the Shadow," and we love it, though oft we may not see the way clearly through tear-dimmed eyes, yet we cry out in our anguish, " Not my will, Father, but thine be done ! " And then " the Shadow " reveals its mystery and departs, leaving the heart chastend and lightened with increased purity and peace. We are cast down in order that we may go higher. Thus, alternately cast down and exalted, we are prepared to meet all the changes of this mundane life. No stoic can be a Rosicrucian : it requires *feeling*, and that intensified. Without this, no initiation could possibly impart that baptism of the spirit which gives birth to new or dormant energies, or awakens soul germs of a higher and better life, where *will* reigns over all, and matter becomes transmutable.

Who are Rosicrucians? I may answer, " By their fruits

shall ye know them." No better test, or one more unerring or unmistakable could be given than that given by
our Master, "the man of Sorrows" whom they hanged on a
CROSS long ago. Let others speak for themselves! There is
nothing in Rosicruciæ to be ashamed of, and I glory in
being one, though an *humble builder of the Temple* in
these degenerate times. There are many pretenders—but
"by their fruits shall ye know them." But fruits are not
always confined to acts. They are visible to the acute
sense, even in the embryo, in the spirit, as fruit may be
known in a tree by its buds. I meet many Rosicrucians,
and although total strangers, we know each other at sight.
The true artist has a *feeling which transcends his thought
in viewing works of art.* It is his best and safest guide
to a just and true estimate of what he beholds. GOD
fashions all things and paints them in all colors possible.
There is nothing in existence that is not of kin to intelligence. They are all suggestive of thought—nay! *they
are thoughts materialized.* And He has fashioned men
with thought-reservoirs, as a flower, for receiving the
polen and the dew; and the Rosicrucian may be known
by the stamp that GOD has put upon him, whether he is
conscious of it or not.

Men who have existed on this earth previous to this
existence, *as men*, have forms, expression and motion more
suggestive of peace, rest and harmony than those who
have only just commenced life on this planet. The former have more receptiveness, prescience, and intuition;
for they have not wholly forgotten the lessons learned in
other bodies; neither have they entirely forgotten the

friends and companions of that other life; and when they meet they feel a mutual attraction and friendship for each other—a *kindred* feeling, more real than that of the blood.

During my studies of nature, and my travels as a lecturer and practitioner of phrenology and kindred sciences, I have met with many men, and many strange—and, I might say, weird—experiences. I have looked into eyes of all shades of color that *contained nothing*, but which reflected all the phenomenon of the outer world. Other eyes I have met that looked deep—as into a world of causation, without limit—as looking into an eternal past, and out of which rises up shadows, not dark or many colored, but fiery, as it were, or of a burning, melting tenderness. Such shadows are portents of power. Of such are Rosicrucians. Many such have I taught the true principles of human life and action, and sent them on their way rejoicing. Many a false step have I arrested, and infused hope into the minds of the desperate—aye! and turned the would-be suicide into the ways of love, labor and usefulness. The evil is always too apparent in the young: the good is mainly hidden. To find the truly good in the soul, and display it to the consciousness, is to make it loved and followed as a beacon of life. The will needs an incentive, high and noble, in order to its growth; and no matter how lofty one's own ideal of himself and his powers may be, to find them recognized by another, and that other a stranger, is like doubling the powers to its attainment. Alas! how many of mature years are in doubt and condemnation of themselves, because they are not, and never have been, understood, *i. e.*, the *best part of themselves.* We long to have the good of ourselves understood, and not the evil. There is a faculty in the soul that causes strangers to recognize each other as friends. Once upon a time, more than a score of years ago, in a Western city, as I walked along seeing and hearing nothing, I met a young man—a mere youth. Why I should have looked at him, and he at me, as we met, is an unsolved mystery. We mutually recognized each other, and yet we were total strangers in the flesh. This chance-meeting led to a mutual friendship. We often met for conversation, and I learned that he was a medical student struggling up into nature's mysteries unaided and alone, thinking to solve the mysteries of humanity by studying the various branches of medicine. I gazed into his pale face and lustrous eyes, tinged with a shade of sadness, and I read there an enthusiastic nature, toned down with logic and doubt; a soul all luminous with the merit of a past eternity, but loaded down with chains forged of doubt. I saw a temperament, strong, sensitive and flexible; and an intellect deep, comprehensive, analytical and subtle, owing its main power to an intuitive perception which ruled all the rest. His mind was so nicely balanced and poised, that to fix his thought intently upon one subject for a brief space of time was enough to open his soul to an influx of light, an unerring guide to truth and the right relation of things. This combination would, I perceived, make him an adept in the diagnosis of disease and the selection of the best remedies therefor. His countenance would glow with a weird and mysterious light as I talked with him of the Rosy Cross, and then the doubt would lower his look, the exaltation disappear, and the fiery shadows of his glance change to a dark hue. But I conversed long and earnestly with him, for it seemed to us both that we had known each other in a previous existence. And I was anxious to impart to him the knowledge I had gained on these subjects, and demonstrate to him that the science of Rosicruciæ containd all the powers he sought : and I am satisfied he profited by my labors. I pictured for him a glorious future in the manifestation of a power of healing of disease superior to any known in modern times, and a fame that would immortalize his name. We parted : he to go East, and I to my wandering. Years fled away, and I heard little or nothing of him, till in 1869 or 1870, a remarkable cure that he had effected was reported in the *Banner of Light*. It seems that a council of physicians had given the patient (who had been under treatment several weeks) up to die, stating that death would take place by midnight of that day ; as a last hope my young friend was called in at 8 o'clock P. M., and before the fatal midnight came the patient was *cured*, and made "every whit whole." At last here was a verification of the truth of my predictions in part, and I watched anxiously for more. The next I heard of him he was professor in some medical college. Then I sat down and grieved over him. I was sad ; for "no man can serve GOD and "*Drugs*" at the same time ! "

Time was when man had more faith in the Gods than in physical substances, and diseases were prevented and cured by the use of talismans, incantations, invocations, words, thoughts, spells, charms, etc., all of which were mere forms of expression for that spiritual power of which I have spoken, having an effect upon the mind primarily, and secondarily upon the body. But man's spiritual nature has gradually become more and more dense, or physical, and instead of carrying or wearing talismans, charms, etc., as a protection or cure, people now invoke the doctors instead of the gods, and swallow their amulets whole at a gulp ; and yet people die now as then, or as when MOSES set up the brazen serpent in the wilderness.

GOTTAMA said that the most fatal diseases enter through the eye ; and we of the ROSY CROSS know this is true ; for through the eye the imagination (in most men) is fed, and the passions may be aroused to the commission of acts unhallowed and unnatural. By reason of which the soul is tainted with moral poison, which in the blood produces venereal infections, hereditary and deadly—the foundation of all known diseases. If disease enters ever, or in any form whatever, through the eye, it cannot be removed by agents which act upon the physical or chemical organization only, for the reason, it being of a spiritual or psychical origin, it enters directly into and deranges the harmonious action of the spiritual body, which holds supreme control over the physical. To cure these phases of disease the remedies applied must be of a character that will influence directly the subtle, spiritual forces of the individual, and through them produce vital and chemical changes in the physical structure. After the cure above referred to, effected by my friend, I heard nothing of him for some time, and I feared he had devoted himself wholly to materialistic science, and ignored his intuitive and spiritual powers ; but ere long I learned to the contrary, for an account of another of his astonishing cures—which materialism never could effect—was published throughout the States: that of Rev. G. W. Enders, an eminent divine of the Lutheran denomination. The *Lutheran Observer*, of Philadelphia, Pa., contained the history of Mr. Enders's case, and of his cure, which was so remarkable that a controversy resulted between Rev. Mr. Enders, Rev. Mr. Lake, and others who were acquainted with all the particulars, on one side, and on the other by a number of "D. D.'s" and "M. D.'s" who knew nothing of the case, but who criticized the publication over the signature of clergymen, of a cure effected by means "not universally recognized and accepted by science and experience," as expressed by them. When I read these articles I rejoiced for my friend, for I realized he had not forsaken his birth-right of power for a mess of scientific pottage : though he is a true scientist and his powers are based upon laws as scientific and permanent as universe. I may here state, the publication in the *Lutheran Observer* of Rev. Enders's cure was a necessary result or sequence of preceding references which it had frequently made, relative to Mr. Enders's condition during the years of his illness, up to the week previous to his cure, at which time he was reported dying. This being followed in a few days by the news of his complete restoration to health, naturally created surprise and doubt, and inquiries from friends and acquaintances in all parts of the country.

In referring to this cure, as one of the many as remarkable effected by the same physician, I can be but brief
and give only a few points from the published statements
made by Rev. Enders, the patient, and other clergymen.
He had been an invalid for years ; was paralyzed, and given
up as hopeless by several physicians previous to entering
the medical institute, where he grew worse until the
physician-in-chief of the establishment telegraphed to his
friends that he was dying, and also dispatched to Philadelphia for my friend, the physician who eventually restored
him to perfect health.   When he arrived, being an entire
stranger to the patient as well as the physicians, he made no
explanation of what he designed to do, but after examining
the case, placed his hands upon MR. ENDERS's head and
bade him ''arise and walk,'' which he did, and continues
so to do to this day, as I have taken pains to ascertain,
and is fulfilling his mission as a religious teacher.   Whence
came this power and this life?—from the Doctor ? Nay,
but from HEAVEN, the source and great reservoir of life.
Did the heavens open especially at this man's bidding to
shower a blessing especially upon the Rev. Mr. Enders?
No ! but the soul of the Doctor opened wide its portals,
being moved by sympathy, and life flowed into the Doctor
and out of his hands into MR. ENDERS, who evidently
was spiritually receptive.   Heaven is always ready to
shower its choicest blessings upon a great soul whenever
it will rise up to receive it.   Heaven never bends down
to us—we must rise up to it in order to receive its
blessings.

This was, I think, in 1876, and the press of the East teemed with accounts, discussions, and efforts to explain the *modus operandi* by which he performed such wonderful results; and some foreign papers also gave accounts of his mysterious cures. Numerous were the efforts made to explain away these marvelous cures, or, at least, to destroy their supernatural appearance. The religious were divided: some said it was of the "Devil;" others, ascribing his power to the HOLY GHOST; while the so-called scientific squelched out the marvelousness of it by crying out those stereotyped but meaningless words: "magnetism, humbug, imagination, etc." How satisfying mere *names* are to most men. Some persons when estimating these extraordinary powers possessed by this physician to relieve suffering and cure disease, deem it either the result of acquired skill or some secret of "magnetism," etc., which could be imparted to another in words. How far such minds are from comprehending the true nature of the principles of Rosicrucia!

Let those who seek to enter these so-called mysteries here learn of their nature, and know they are reached only by *power of soul*—so often gained through its agony and travail that gives it "birth into the higher mysteries."

As the world will be prone to misapprehend the source of the principles and the powers of the soul which I have pointed out as belonging to the Rosicrucian mysteries, I will endeavor to show their highest development to be an expression of soul-growth through discipline and suffering; and, to do so, have referred to my friend's experience; for, though that friend and I have met only

on one occasion since a score of years ago, and have
corresponded but very rarely, I have watched his life-line,
and find it in the actual the same as it was so vividly
portrayed to me in prevision in the long-passed years
when he and I conversed on the subject of these hidden
and subtle powers of the soul. In that long ago, I perceived the key-note of his nature and of his greatest future
trial—that which would bring to him the shadow, or
rather bring his soul to that shadowy guardian of the
temple's portal, with which he would contend to obtain
. spiritual powers.

His theory then, in those his youthful days was, that
"each individual is but the half of a complete soul until
it meets its counterpart—its true companion; and that
neither man nor woman can be truly great, spiritually or
intellectually, before that true union is formed." To this
I would reply, " None can be truly great *until they have
suffered.*"

I realized his belief on this subject was a fundamental
element of his nature, and perceived it would be the rock
upon which his earthly hopes would be wrecked.

Ten years thereafter, being in Philadelphia, I visited
my friend of the long ago,* and luckily found him at
home. He had recently taken to himself a wife, but
his mind was occupied in his profession of medicine
and surgery; for, indeed, he travels far and wide in
response to calls to visit the so-called hopelessly sick.
To the far West, the extreme South, North and East he is
no stranger; and thousands bless his name. But space
bids me hasten to a close. We passed a pleasant time

---

* J. J. Jones, M. D., Philadelphia, Pa.

together in cheerful reminiscences of the past and in con-
jectures of the future.

When I referred to his old-time belief on the subject
of "true mating" and true greatness, he replied, "Oh!
this is a practical world, and we cannot allow the romance
of our natures to govern us through this life; you see I
have a companion and home, and am trying to fulfil my
life-mission by relieving suffering; ought I not be satisfied?" But I saw he was living only the half of his nature—
the material, or as he would express it, the "practical."
His companion was a lady of fine education, but seemed
to possess none of the high aspirations that would have
been congenial to her husband's nature. Another more
fatal source of dread, I soon discovered in the fact that
she was a victim to the morphine habit. My friend ac-
knowledged this, but spoke hopefully of redeeming her
from the habit; he was sanguine of success, because at
that time he did not know the habit was of many years'
duration.

When my short but pleasant visit was terminated, he
accompanied me to the train. As I clasped his hand and
looked in his kind, hopeful eyes, I saw their light flicker and
go out, leaving a shadow as of night. I was so moved that
I could only gasp out, " Good-bye, my old friend! God
bless you!" And then I left him with the shadow clinging
to me. Seated in the cars, I looked at my watch and
then settled myself to study the shadow, but it revealed
nothing—not even his face. The train whirled on, and
time whirled away into eternity, until at the end of ten
hours the shadow began to dissipate, and his face seemed

to emerge therefrom, a shade paler, with the lines deepened, and a look with the same fire in it, but the boyish enthusiasm toned down. The setting sun shone for a moment, ere it sunk to rest, upon his upturned face, which was radiant with a spiritual light, and turning his old look upon me he said, "We live for eternity, not merely for a day or a few weary years. What is a little time, or a small shadow of ten years?" And then he disappeared, and the shadow was gone and my heart was light again. Shortly after, I came South and lost sight of him; but in time I learned that the shadow had fallen upon him, as I had seen it in my vision. That nameless, shapeless monster "guardian of the threshold" of power had hurled him down—not from his fame, his manhood, nor his power—but from his enthusiam, his hopes of earthly happiness, and his ambition to gain the world's approval.

But "Rosicrucians never fail" is an adage among them; for that which appears as a failure in the eyes of other men, they look upon as a stepping stone to something higher and better. Everything has its uses, and they always look for the use of what appears an evil. Every soul of worth must be tried and tested, and they that rise up out of deep sorrow, purified and made better, have received nature's stamp of salvation; for the spirit of nature never errs in the "selection of the fittest" to do its work in the intellectual and spiritual as well as in the physical realm.

To pass this dark shadow, this "guardian of the threshold," the nameless, shapeless monster, to which "despair" is but a faint definition, was the ordeal my friend was ordained to undergo, as do all others who enter the temple of spiritual power and wisdom.

Those who have native strength of spirit to pass the ordeal, have power not only to save themselves, but to help others to salvation; while those who have not, are crushed as bubbles by the wind, and disappear, never more to be known on earth. My friend did not disappear, but with a stoical and dogged resolution plodded on his cheerless and desolate way, dispensing health to the sick and hope to the hopeless; he was always busy; but whether by night or by day, in his office or by the bedside of the sick, at home or flying with the speed of steam for thousands of miles at the call of the suffering; that monster shadow never left his sight; but, amid all, he had a firm belief and an "abiding faith" in his destiny; and he cast about in his mind for ways to defeat this thing that had impeded his flight; but all the approaches to "the threshold" were guarded by this nameless thing.

At last there sounded in his soul—as if coming from afar—these words: "Resist not evil; but use it—learn of it." And forthwith he set himself to learn this lesson: that evil is at the foundation of everything, and he that would transcend it must build *thereon*—not ignore it, nor treat it as an enemy and foe to human happiness, greatness and power. Evil is a friend in disguise. And he learned the deep lesson—that this monster shadow of the soul, this guardian of the mysteries, is an enemy only to those hopes and ambitions that pertain to this, the earthly phase of life; and, while it crushes those whose lives are

centred on these selfish hopes and ambitions, to those
whose earthly hopes are destroyed and lives made desolate, and who still remain strong in spirit, it becomes an
angel of light, a messenger of joy from the inner sanc-
tuary of divine love.

This dreaded power that hovers between the world
material and the realm of spirit ever meets those whom
nature has ordained shall pass the ordeal during earth-
life, by bringing its terrible powers to bear upon and
destroy the strongest sentiment of that soul that would
cause it to cling to earth. The dominant worldly passion
or trait of character indicates the point of attack of this
enemy, for it indicates the weakest point in the individual
nature. Those who live for worldly renown are brought
low and made humble ; those who seek wealth are made
poor, and those who would wish to create for themselves
a home of earthly means, by living for its passive or
physical comforts only ; dwelling wholly in their material
nature, at the sacrifice of their ideal or spiritual nature,
are made homeless, and, perhaps, to feel friendless. And
so on, through the gamut of earthly hopes and ambitions,
they each and all must be crushed, ere the soul learns
the great truth that it is now, in the present, *immortal.*
It must be stripped of its selfish and worldly nature ere it
can become strong in its spiritual powers, even as the tree
must be trimmed of its useless branches, let them be ever
so luxurious, ere it can blossom and bring forth good fruit.
These are hard lessons to learn, but my friend learned
them ; and he who truly and practically learns them makes
a servant of the "Devil," and compels him to undo his

own work. The ten years had not passed since I met my friend, when the light began to dawn upon his soul. Gradually the shadow faded away, and he became luminous with hope, faith, renewed youth, and growing power. Already his eye, piercing through the gloom of the early morn, espies afar off the descent of the TEMPLE of the ROSY CROSS—that temple " not made with hands, eternal in the heavens." And methinks I see him don the mystic garments and fearlessly step across the threshold of the inner temple and clasp the outstretched hands of our grand old masters. Oh ! how the soul thrills with joy and veneration when, in our mystic scroll, we read the history of those mighty minds of the past. Those sublime masters, Hermes-Trismagistus (thrice master), Gottama, Appolonius of Tyane, Pythagoras, Anaxagoras, Socrates, Zoroaster, and Jesus, down through the vista of time, including Cornelius Agrippa, Robert Flood, and the host of others in whose great souls burn the same divine fire : yet the world knows them not. Meek and lowly as men, misunderstood and rejected by the bigoted and ignorant masses, they lived in the light and joy of the higher life. Though persecuted and crucified, they never knew of death, for they had gained immortality while yet in the flesh, and, casting aside of the old garments of clay, only added strength and wisdom to their mental powers. As they were persecuted and crucified by ignorance and bigotry, under the name of religion, so also were they, in a later day, "deified" by the same elements of selfish ignorance, and their true power and glory hidden from mankind under the black cowl of religious tyranny. Notwithstanding this dark pall of gloom thrown over their names, their living presence permeates every fibre of the world, and their spiritual influence is felt in the moral atmosphere of reform, which, in its various phases, is ever active to exalt, purify and ennoble mankind.

Readers, many of you have felt the divine influence of these grand old masters of the Rosy Cross, and were you to lay aside your doubt and egotistic pride, and let your souls become receptive, you, too, would receive power to bless your fellow creatures, to bring health to the sick, hope to the despairing, and the joyous knowledge of *immortality* to those faltering ones who deem the *grave* God's last gift to man. "Try!"

Blessed is he who believes from the force of evidence, but thrice blessed is he who believes *without* evidence.

Lovingly, for the world, written :

F. B. DOWD.

THE
TEMPLE OF THE ROSY CROSS.

THE SOUL:

ITS POWERS, MIGRATIONS, AND TRANSMIGRATIONS.

By F. B. DOWD.

PHILADELPHIA:

John R. Rue, Jr., Printer, No. 43 South Fourth Street.

—1882.—